Preface

We are facing some mighty big problems. WE MUST WAKE UP! The solutions will come by through individuals who have transcended post-modern ways of thinking, addressing questions in terms of the highest and best good for all involved. How do we avoid falling into the abyss? The good news is, we are really speeding up. The bad news is, despite valiant attempts to impose a counter-narrative, we are still in great peril, and we have to act quickly. This is your news report. It's the first of three books designed to convince US that WE CAN AND MUST WAKE UP!!! I'm writing it because I can. I don't have a marketing budget, so if you've read this, you are now part of this never-ending story. If you are still stuck IN THE BLATANT AND OBVIOUS TRAP OF A PARADIGM, you can wait 'til at least two books are out, and then read it.

The You'll have some catching up to do…

That impulse, the one you feel to check for permission, is a clear example of false subconscious programming. It's your life. It's your mind. It's your body. Tell them to shove their authority up their ass.

So… I have a slight confession…. I staged another version of this book and published it under the name Chery E. Goetz-Ward. It had some valuable insights, and I was a little meaner than I am in this version to my former employers, but(in my opinion) they are assholes, and I knew for sure that they would read this before anyone else. There were a few errors, and they bought most of the copies that have been sold. It was priced WAY too high, and I have just removed it to go off into the woods to die (not really)

I'm not going to link this book to my name or Cheryl's. I'm going to target it to younger generations and make the cover quite unappealing to stuffy assholes.

For the future thinkers and future leaders among you, I think you're going to enjoy this

It may be possible to write a book describing the process and pitfalls associated with waking up in more natural terms, but this is the best I could come up with.

In an attempt to make this a more leisurely read, Cheryl Goetz-Ward will be commenting along the way to help ensure that I explain things, well, as clearly as possible.

Cheryl's comments/questions will be underlined. I tried several different ways to incorporate her. <u>Underlining</u>, while a little stiff, was the best solution for both paperback and Kindle formats.

When I was a child, my father told me one of his favorite jokes, "Son, there are only three kinds of *fair* in this world.

       1) County Fair
       2) State Fair
       3) World's Fair

"

There's way too much truth in there to make it the least bit funny, any more. Can I please help you change it?

Promises

This is not a theology report. Well, I guess it sort of is, but If you allow it to be, it will also be a doorway.

<u>"More of this?"</u>

The answer is, "Yes, and no." It will be different, starting now: I will not make a confusing or ambiguous statement without explaining it in a way that can be understood with common logic.

This is an excellent time to tell you that I LAUGH A LOT. To make sure this keeps the *most productive tone possible*. When I notice it, I'll try to chuckle in print.

<u>"Hmm? I suppose that sounds alright… for now, IF you tell me how the answer can be yes, and no? I hate when you self-described Gurus drop riddles like that and move on."</u>

Very fair. I'm not a guru. The nature of reality is that higher truths often seem paradoxical.

Yes, it is "more of this," but only in terms of the fact that this book will address *topics* that you may be familiar with. No… In fact, hell no, *it is not* going to be a retread. That's what I meant when I told you this would not be a report. This will not be the same information that you have read elsewhere unless it is given as a starting point, to create something new, by either expansion, revision, or clarification.

> "You want me to read a book, by someone whom I've never heard of, that endeavors to improve the work of Ramana Maharshi and Nisargadatta Maharaj?"

Don't forget the Bible. (chuckle) I'm going to improve on that too.

> "I don't believe you. At all…but I am intrigued."

Good! Go with that! It matters not why you read this! You shouldn't accept ANYTHING YOU READ OR HEAR as accurate unless you *realize* that it is! No woo there. This is the definition I was implying:

> **realize**: become fully aware of (something) as a fact; understand clearly.

> "To quote Whitney Houston, how will I know?"

> That's the spirit!

I think William Shakespeare said it best… *Aye; There's the rub.* I can assure you I had no idea either, but that part has not been a struggle. It has always been apparent to me. I may not have, metaphorically, seen the stone before I started stepping, but it was always there when I landed. This is my reasoning. Hence, if I ask you to follow exactly where I climbed, the stones are still there, and it is a relatively safe path. If you're unstable, and this book has just been released, it might be a good idea to give it as a gift, first. (chuckle) That was a joke, but there's a grain of truth in it.

> "Between that and the vampire reference, this is getting dangerously close to narcissism. Some De-Wooing is in order."

> Understandable.

As I grew in awareness, I frequently contemplated the nature of reality, and I started being able to span more and more logical steps at a time. It was as though because I had established a rock-solid orientation of intention, I could take longer and longer strides into the unknown before touching down at a point that either seemed right or at least accurate enough to support while I reordered the logic to make the platform more stable. I suppose it was a little like the Olympic sport of curling. As far as the narcissism comment, it gets worse before it gets better. (chuckle) I think that the ability that I have just described is the essence of genius, and I'm reasonably sure that's correct.

<u>"You're on thin ice."</u>

Count me warned.

Let's play with the image we're using to understand that process… Picture each steppingstone as one step in a series of building epiphanies. In feeling terms, the term *"aha* moment" works pretty well for describing what it feels like when each stepping stone first appears. After the "Aha!" the most recent stone is only able to support the weight of one foot. Metaphorically, a more accurate way of describing it would be to say that the step or platform first appears a semi-stable pile of steppingstone pieces. Now, when each "step kit" appears, I know it wouldn't have done so UNLESS it contained a complete platform. However, when I would attempt to place too much of my weight there, the stone pile would begin to wobble. Sometimes, I had to leap backward and pull myself up onto the previous stepping stone with both hands.

It is for this reason, out of caution, that there will be a few places in the book where I believe it would be unwise to stop reading.

<u>"So, you're a vampire, and your book might make me crazy? Any other reason I should stop reading now and run, or is that it, because…"</u>

Picture me smiling at you with kind eyes.

I haven't fallen yet, and I am planning to show you as much of my path as I can. It is my reasonable expectation that, for many, it will be a more familiar, and more complete path than you have encountered before. Think of me as a beggar trying to show another beggar where I have found bread.

<u>"Cute."</u>

Be nice.

This is where it gets a little tricky. I have come to understand that, unless your strides are as long as mine, I can't bring you with me by simply stepping forward and describing the next platform. I realize that everything I have said is hard to take on faith, but if you allow me to stretch the metaphor just a little further, I can explain how I might point you to a similar path that requires... less.

"How?"

By doing this…

Although what I would call discovery points would only appear while striding forward, if I looked back carefully, I noticed that I could clarify the realization in a way that seemed to create a straight path to follow. It should be noted that I was only able to see alternate routes emerge AFTER the discovery point *had been assembled, positioned, oriented, balanced, and secured.*

This book is my utmost attempt to step forward, call to you from the direction of each discovery point, and then point out the more natural path.

I will lead a path through the mist that allows a sincere, balanced seeker to safely follow.

The Seeker's Uniform

I don't want to be above you. I don't want to be above anyone. I pray every day for God to allow me to be the lowest of all, but unafraid.

"Why would you want to be *less than?*"

That's exactly what I thought the first time I read a prayer containing the verbiage, *"allow me to see myself as the lowest of all."*

I can see now that I was dead wrong, and this attitude is crucial.

I currently pray for God to allow me to *be* the lowest of all, but to mean that I had to fist pray often for God to let me *see myself that way.*   More experienced seekers may disagree with that progression, and they have a point. (chuckles) The reason that *seeing myself* as the lowest of all is important is that it negates the *perceived* obligation to declare judgment.

<u>"Obligation?"</u>

That word does seem to be correct.

Don't we judge as if it's our job? Think about it. Why do we do that? Don't ask, *why do I think I do that?* Here's a better question… *Is there an understanding of the universe that makes the judgment that just arose both unneeded and unhelpful?*

My favorite restaurant is called *The Bubble Room.* It is a whimsical, magical place *on Captiva Island, FL.* The she-crab soup, prime rib, and outrageously large dessert cake slices are legendary, and it has toy trains running around the ceiling of every room. There are Christmas decorations galore, including some enjoyable bubble lights. The dining tables are display cases filled with memorabilia, spanning everything from old advertisements and records to nostalgic game pieces that capture the essence of childhood. My favorite place to sit is in any of the booths along the fish-tank wall on the second floor.

<u>"Why?"</u>

I like the fish tank, though they are deceptive.

In an alcove on the way to the second-floor dining room, they have a mechanical Macy's Christmas window display from the early 1900s that still functions. The servers there are unique. They introduce themselves as "Bubble Scouts." Captiva Island, itself, is beautiful and relaxing, but a getaway weekend there isn't complete without a night at The Bubble Room. I will leave the details of their uniforms for you to experience freshly, for yourself, but they help to create an atmosphere that should be experienced at least once.

<u>"…but how were you tricked by fish tanks?"</u>

First, you were also, but in a way that is true with ANY finite system.

We have a collective hubris that makes it so. We, humans, have a tendency to mentally partition what we see from the overall system and assume that the rules we deduce by watching the partition apply to the whole.

We do this in at least two ways that can be explained using a fish tank as an example. If we see 5 different individual examples of fish species in a partitioned section, we get a different picture of fish behavior and fish identity than we would if we saw them swimming in schools. We can not deduce fish schools from that example of a fish tank. We do not know what we do not know when analyzing a fixed system. That is the basis for many confusing "yes, and no" woo-ish answers. If you notice, most of the setups for those answers are questions like is the bluefish with the yellowtail an individual? With no other information, the most correct answer is yes and no. No woo.

I think Walt Whitman, who is different than Walt Disney…

> "Hey!"

…was alluding to this concept in his famous quote, "Do I contradict myself? Very well, then. I contradict myself. I am large. I contain multitudes."

I have some strange… well… conditions. I am beautifully broken. I won't tell you what I mean just yet. That choice is not about me. Never about me. Every word is for you.

I have become integrated, but it hasn't been easy.

This is an accurate description of the iterations that I go through.

> First, my higher Self intuits a concept, on purpose and my egoic voice either agrees or abstains from *the discussion.*

> "Which one? Agrees or abstains?"

> Keep doing that.

I think it agrees, but I can't be sure. How could I know? I don't take jumps in logic. I don't accept anything as given. I can deduce from the fact that there are only two forms of thought present in my awareness that it is either one or the other. I don't notice much "monkey mind" chatter, and interruptions in my train of thought are rare.

> "Monkey Mind?"

> "Egoic voice? …NOT A RETREAD?"

Keen observations. I'm guessing the question pertains to the implied premise.

It does seem paradoxical at first. I have an ego, complete with an egoic voice, but I AM NOT that ego? If that's true, and it is, then it DOES FOLLOW that I am also NOT THE BODY.

<u>"WTF? Give me my money back, woo peddler."</u>

Not so fast. I believe I can explain it in a way that makes logical sense.

Has anyone else EVER done that to your satisfaction?

Seriously, have they? I've read or listened to many, many spiritual and religious books, and I haven't found it. Not externally. Just so you know exactly what you're in for, I am going to make you a few promises:

1) I promise that ALMOST EVERYTHING that sounds… Woo-ish or Woo-like won't remain that way. If it does, I believe it must.
2) I promise to be kind, but in a way that keeps you interested.
3) I promise to make sense.
4) I promise to explain why gurus often *don't make sense.*

It's not just that they won't. I believe many can't. Let me ask you this: If I levitate over an obstacle course and choose not to look down, am I an expert at obstacle courses? Why?

From the perspective of where they find themselves the moment they begin to think linearly again, it's nearly IMPOSSIBLE to INFER the path. That's unfortunate because, from the perspective of the seeker, a description of the guru's current view is otherwise of little value.

5) I promise that waking up is very real and very possible.
6) I promise not to fuck with you… for more than a moment.

<u>"Thank you."</u>

<u>I pinky swear on that one.</u>

"Nice."

I am dumbfounded at what I hear some gurus say and ask. The inescapable conclusion is that some of them are missing large chunks of understanding and, sadly, many of them are total frauds. Their belief that nothing can or should change, or be done, is a fallacy akin to, "my vote doesn't matter."

Our definition of enlightenment as a homogenous category should change. I am not placing myself above gurus. What I would like is for us to all move forward from here, together.

7) I promise you that I have risen above conditioned-thinking.
8) I promise that I can easily hold my attention in one place for more than five minutes.
9) I promise that if you read every word of this book, at the very least, you will be smarter, more virtuous, and less fearful.
10)   I promise that every word I write will be carefully chosen.
11)   I promise that I believe every word in this book to be truthful.
12)   I believe there are masters in this world, who can neutralize large amounts of negative energy by radiating love and positive thoughts. It's awesome. Truly awesome.
13)   I am incredibly optimistic about what lies ahead.
14)   This book will make narrow-minded people very angry and could very well stir some heinous shit, WHICH IS NEEDED AT THIS TIME.
15)   After I have given you everything that I know, I will entertain you with a whitewashed version of my story, and some exciting ideas on how and when some of our religious conventions may have originated. The circumcision one made me do my best Homer Simpson impersonation.

Are You Enlightened?

Well… I am not continuously in a state of mystical union, though I have glimpsed it on a few occasions. I don't want to be. It feels great and all, but I am not in this for the bliss ride. Until I have bendy-strawed this and a few other ideas into consensus reality, I believe it would be counterproductive. For most of this life, I have (mis) understood that spiritual truths could not be explained or grasped using language or linear logic. I really, really thought that was true. The best answer I can give you is… enlightened enough, ma'am or sir.

I had read it repeatedly. Haven't you? I have read many times that profound spiritual truths cannot be communicated via words.

I was not yet polarized to the positive, as I am now, so I wasn't secure enough to question. It's not true, but it is *almost right.* The explanation for higher truth, in my case anyway, must be deduced while the entire concept is present in my awareness. Holding complicated pieces of a disjointed framework in my awareness long enough to map them onto a cohesive frame isn't something that I used to be able to do.

"But you can now?"

Yes.

"Cool."

I know.

"Were all those masters lying?"

I don't think so.

First, it's not a homogenous category. Some were. In addition to the fakers, I have encountered a few gurus along my journey I would describe as genuine, but so inept that the term "blind following the blind" may have come into existence on their behalf. One particular Facebook guru really LOOKED like the real deal, gray dreads and all, but I was shocked! Shocked, I tell you… when I read his responses. I think he was *trolling me.*

To end this chapter on a positive note, one living sage I AM SURE is far beyond most others is named Sadhguru, which ironically translates to "uneducated guru." As an ordinary noun, the word sadhguru is sometimes also used to refer to our "inner guru," which is the voice inside of each of us that WE CAN access in stillness.

Tim & Old Bob's Reality Tunnels

The term reality tunnel was created by Timothy Leary and built upon by

Robert Anton Wilson. In *Prometheus Rising,* I think Old Bob (term of endearment) got it right.

Leary founded the League for Spiritual Discovery, which he defined as a religious movement "dedicated to the ancient sacred sequence of turning on, tuning it, and dropping out."

Here is Wikipedia's definition:

Reality tunnel is a theory that, with a subconscious set of mental filters formed from beliefs and experiences, every individual interprets the same world differently, hence "Truth is in the eye of the beholder."

I would add a word. Relative. I don't believe all truth is in the eye of the beholder(s). From a wide range of perspectives, though sometimes only temporarily, some claims can be proven to be universally true.

> "If all that exists are reality tunnels, How can any truth be absolute?"

> First, that's a good question.

> Second, I never said that reality tunnels are all that exist. I told you they do exist. Big difference. Let's take a moment, so misunderstandings like that happen as little as possible.

Every word in this book will be truthful. A few on the cover are made up (*the name*). In the interest of full transparency, *I can* foresee that some of you will make assumptions about me. A more accurate description would be, your body, which you believe to be you, will automatically feed you bullshit, whether your higher self wants it to or not.

Again, what "you" have always considered to be *you* is incomplete at best. You may have felt like a "legion." But you can be 2. The ego will loosen its grip, and as soon as you gain control, God will guide you internally. There is a simple, rational understanding of God that still butts up against a complete mystery.

Please pay careful attention here: Have you read the Cherokee story about us all having two wolves inside? The black wolf is your ego. It's not bad, but it's caught in quite a tangle. It keeps eating every time you IDENTIFY with a selfish thought.

> In this instance, rather than having the sense that you have "observed a series of thoughts," you instead feel as if *YOU thought them.*

As soon as you place a small amount of distance between what you absolutely know to be accurate and your interrupting thoughts, everything will begin to unravel.

I'll rephrase that, because it *is vitally important,* the first step in getting off of the merry go round is to allow ideas to happen and to observe them without it feeling like it's something YOU DID. When I made that shift, "I" became Self and self. Many became two. For a while, anyway.

I intend to help as many humans as I can, as much as I can. Come what may. Please tell your body to shut up, or at least reserve judgment, rather than holding me accountable for what IT tells you. I'm not tricking you. It is. Again, the body is wrong, not bad. It doesn't know it's wrong. It thinks it's you, and it is acting as such. Constantly.

I share my opinions openly and honestly, and I share them with compassion, but I tend not to respect traditional norms of communication between humans.

> "Why?"

> Because, as I believe I have mentioned, most of you are entirely full of shit. Not all of you, but the committee that's currently in charge sure is.

To put it nicely, your reality tunnel seems immovable. Unless I can find a way to change several beliefs at the same time, we're destined for a futile game of whack-a-mole.

Which Wei?

> "No spell check?"

Wei, as in Wu Wei, which means without forcing. It is a term Zen Masters use to describe their state of mind. One of the best definitions I have ever heard for Wu Wei is simply: Sleep when tired. Eat when hungry. The reason I feel that is accurate is this: When you are down to one fuck given, you don't care what people think. Established, accepted solutions can, independently, have very little truth.

I have watched endless hours of YouTube and read some incredible books. I research to amass data points to use for inference. Of course, I don't summarily discount every conclusion, but I don't accept them, either. My mind is open to everything and attached to nothing. Not my words, but it fits. Pick an acknowledged, consensus sage at random and attribute it to them.

I do not let *what anyone else says*, "*Cannot be*" distract me from realizing *what is*. That means you should be prepared to rationally consider some bizarre shit from diverse perspectives, in a way that is shame free. Are you honestly capable of doing that yet? Would you like to?

Back to reality tunnels… there are individual reality tunnels, which start off way off course, and then there is a *more* absolute reality. Relative truths can be built on assumptions. Higher truths can be apprehended only by carefully studying principles and data points that are experientially true, across a wide range of individual reality tunnels (often misinterpreted), then working sequentially forward or backward using other *more* absolute truths, some of which are mysteries. Many things we collectively consider to be true simply can't be.

One of the most useful books I have read is the New Living Translation of the Bible. What did Moses hear/sense/intuit on Mt. Sinai? That' right… concerning the roots of Abrahamic religions, I AM THAT I AM is the name of God.

I take full responsibility for accurately describing the map, starting points, starting orientations, and the highest understanding I possess at this moment.

Why This Way?

Why a book? Because your ego/body doesn't just interrupt you; it also interrupts me. A simple conversation wherein I am legitimately trying to help you can feel like traversing a minefield. People don't know why they do what they do most of the time. That's true. I watch you in slow motion.

"Creepy."

Expected, padawan, but false. We have to re-arrange our belief system. For over a year, I have been laser-focused on placing this life support mask on myself, first. It's your turn.

In book form, I can go over what I have written, again and again, and release it when I sense it is strong enough, and clear enough, to help you. You see, I have very few worldly possessions. The *body* that my human father *thought he was* is no more. He chose to leave us. He quite literally sacrificed himself so that my stepmother would no longer have to worry about survival needs. He had a term life policy, about to expire, that he had purchased before he lost everything in the great recession. In the state he lived in, policies must pay out on suicide after 2 years, unless it can be proven that it was planned when it was purchased. That's a just law, by *the way*. I say that knowing full well that my Dad might still be here, but for its existence.

"Isn't that a little much? If you're scared, say you're scared."

The minefield metaphor? I don't think so.

I don't think it is either inaccurate or too firm, and I did not feel fear when contemplating how I might have the best chance of reaching the most people. What's that? Miscommunication won't kill you? In a few pages, if you pay careful attention, you will have the realization, for yourself, that you are not the body. Then we can discuss what "killing you" means in the same language.

I don't say, "you" to place myself above you... I don't want to control you. Quite the contrary. I want to serve you. It may help to look at it this way. I was, in some ways, more human than most. I was DEEP in the mud; I was barely, barely awake. The contrast between how I was then and how I am now is blinding. So much so that I can't, in good conscience, even place it in the same category. I am awake, and that really is the best way to describe it, especially in contrast.

"I can't believe you had the stones to actually write that. You're going to get crucified."

That's ONE of the reasons I asked for your help, Cheryl Goetz-Ward.

Another is that I sense that I am close to another significant realization that transcends and includes my present understanding. There is always a higher understanding. Always. "We" don't have a finish line. I've come a long way. I'm not at all afraid I won't get there. However, the odds that I can help humanity in the future decrease with credit. Good credit OR bad credit (all relative truths). A sleuth could find me, but I ask you to respect my privacy for one year.

<u>"Why write this now, rather than after the next realization?"</u>

A few reasons:

1) Because I can.
2) I have to lower my vibration to write in a way that you can understand. I know that sounds like horseshit, but it's not.
3) When I go a little further, deeper into the woods, I sense I may be able to get from the mental state that I reside in most of the time to a place where I can reach you, but I can't be sure. It's difficult to contact you from here.
4) If I start immediately and insert this into consensus reality, people can read it now, or 50 years from now, and hopefully start waking up to a point where they will be able to connect with "The Holy Spirit(?)" themselves.
5) The lack of connection to spirit in the west is our most significant potential for peril.

<u>"First book?"</u>

That's kind of a funny story. Why do I want to guide you so badly? Because I did not have a guide, and it was painful. Picture someone in a straight jacket, determined to get out. I ran full speed into a lot of walls. I would like to help you avoid some of them. A few of the realizations were, initially, so disturbing that If my Dad had not killed himself, I might have. I think the universe selects for openness and intelligence when choosing a… *is shaman appropriate?*   I claim this because, on several occasions, I needed every bit of my reasoning ability, transparency, and honesty to retreat from madness.

A pause is required. If I don't do some clarification, I can see how that could be misinterpreted as *the big reveal* for you skeptics out there. The exact phrase that came to mind was,

<u>"Enlightened, MY ASS!"</u>

That's the one.

I AM single-minded and plugged into what a lot of people would describe as God, but that is me *today*. I'm a work in progress. On two occasions, after I was able to reside in Self for an extended period, I was thrown back into identification with self. I plan on explaining how it happened and how I found my way again in a chapter called **Potential Pitfalls.**

One of the walls I ran into was… I wrote… (more like channeled) 100 pages in two days. I WAS IN AN ABSTRACT STATE, but still able to transcribe. Since it was so incredible (to me), I saw no problem spending most of my money on clever, short domain names that I could use to create self-sustaining web sites that bring more light into the world. I was out of balance, you see. The thought, "Why on earth would I need to worry about finances when I have just written a masterpiece?" had a lot of holes.

<u>"Well, was it?"</u>

We'll see.

Though still a bit disorganized, with some more work, I think it could be.

It's called "Too Many Pairs," and it's an attempt to rationally get Abrahamic religions to drop their negative stance on homosexual couples. I'll show you the cover in an appendix, but the book is so dense in its current form that it's hard to understand. Initially, I was planning to fold sections into this book and try to water it down, but I have decided to keep this book independent, though there is some overlapping subject matter. As soon as this is published, I will continue that work.

"What are the websites/domains?"

369.care

369.coach
369.expert
4fg.biz
4fg.co
4fg.life
4fg.me
4fg.mobi
4fg.rocks
4fg.shop
4fg.store
4fg.xyz
4free4.fun
4free4.us
4fungod.com
4us.cloud
4us.rocks
9hub.net
9hub.org
9pro.org
allgod.co
allgod.us
allthewaylive.net
amenit.net
amenit.org
amenit.pro
amenit.store
amenit.xyz
arc-angle.com
arcangle.net

artgr.am

artgram.me

artgram.shop

artgram.store

artgram.today

artgram.xyz

bb8.cloud

bb8s.us

beblessed.us

blessit.co

c3p0.co

c3p0.life

c3p0.us

canaa.co

canaa.info

canaa.life

creatoris.love

donttread.us

e-ot.us

ffff-g.com

ffffg.co

ffffg.life

ffffg.me

ffffg.net

ffffg.org

ffffg.space

ffffg.xyz

for1.us

forfreeforfunforgod.com

forfreeforfungod.com

forfungod.co

getgod.us

god-inme.com

godandgod.com

godentered.com

godin.biz

godinme.co

godinme.org

godis-love.com

godis.app

godis.expert

godis.mobi

godis.tv

godis.xyz

godis.zone

godisinlove.com

godislove.cool

godloves.biz

godloves.coffee

godloves.life

godsislove.com

godsolutions.org

godus.love

gogod.us

goodislove.com

grabmethe.net

he-chose.us

heblessed.us

hechose.us

hope4.us

i-4it.com

iam2fit.com

iam9s.com

icandothisallday.com

iget.space

ihorus.xyz

iofus.us

isdavid.com

isus.us

it-ot.us

joy4.us

just9.us

justgod.us

livewithouta.net

luvlove.us

manoflight.xyz

manypair.com

manypair.org

manypairs.space

manypairs.world

me1.us

meal4me.us

meals4.us

my11.us

my9.wine

namedavid.com

nameisdavid.me

nameisdavid.net

nameisdavid.org

nameisdavid.store

newlifewine.com

newwine.biz

newwine.news

newwine.solutions

newwine.xyz

newwine4u.com

newwineus.com

nohands.us

ourdog.us

ourgod.co

ourgod.us

phi-is.com

phiis.co

somethingaboutme.us

tech-ti.com

the5s.us

the9.wine

the9app.com

thearcangle.com

theartgram.com

theartgram.store

thegod.live

themichas.com

theoracleatthisguy.com

thoht.app

thoht.co

thoht.pro

thoht.shop

toomanypairs.com

toomanypairs.info

toomanypairs.net

toomanypairs.org

toomanypairs.us

totwo.us

tri-z-ero.com

trizeros.co

trizeros.com

trizeros.org

trizeros.rocks

trizeros.xyz

tryzeros.co

tryzeros.shop

tryzeros.store

tryzeros.xyz

twbw.co

twbw.me

twbw.store

twbw.xyz

usgod.us

weare.dance

weare.press

weareti.com

x-xn.us

x4us.us

xtwo.us

yahwoh.life

yahwoh.org

yahwoh.shop

yahwoh.us

yahwoh.world

yahwoh.xyz

yahwoo.org

yahwoo.shop

yahwoo.space

yawoh.com

yestheyare.org

you4us.us

yvb.life

yvb.mobi

yvb.today

yvb.world

Taking Steven Pinker's YouTube advice, I have endeavored to write this book from the perspective of the reader. In contrast, the state in which I wrote most of **Too Many Pairs** book could be described as subtle/very subtle. Each idea is expressed in as few sentences as possible. There is little clarification or banter, just pinpoint, pure, undiluted truth, stacked high and narrow, forced through this reality tunnel. I'm going slower this time. The structure is more precise, and I am trying to anticipate questions while always facing in the same direction, building more gradually than before.

    <u>"Are you fucking serious?"</u>

    Do I detect sarcasm?

I'm serious less than I used to be and only when necessary. In this instance, yes. Have you fallen off the cart in an area you didn't recognize? If you think this book is dense, then you should take my point. Relatively, it's cotton candy.

Now, when my mother, who is a brilliant person, proofread THAT book... it didn't go well. FROM MY PERSPECTIVE, IN THAT STATE, little of what she did or said was helpful, or for that matter correct. However, in hindsight, the disconnect at that time ended up being useful. You see, if she had problems understanding it, even though it was logical, I knew I had a lot of work to do to reach a general audience. I'm still optimistic, but cautiously so.

Remember... I had pure intentions, but *I was out of balance* at that time. Since then, a lot has changed. I've settled. Integrated. I have learned not to let ideas raise my level of energy nearly as much. I'm more like Bill Compton than Jessica at the moment.

I was Jessica. Raw mental power. Natural intellect. I was in unfamiliar territory with absolutely no map. I want you to have a map. I want you to have a guide. Fighting with righteous anger and a toothpick is thrilling but ultimately unproductive.

> <u>"You eat people? Drink blood?"</u>
>
>> No, and the sun doesn't burn me. I can't fly. Ironically, THC does seem a little like Trueblood. It helps me when my thinking gets a little too... circular.

That's the other reason I decided to release this anonymously and give Cheryl credit. I live in a state that is still under William Randolph Hearst's evil spell. If you don't know the story... here's the gist... He was a well-respected, successful member of society. HE PUBLISHED HUNDREDS, IF NOT THOUSANDS OF NEWSPAPERS FULL OF ABSOLUTE SELF SERVING LIES about cannabis *to serve his own interest and prohibit hemp from competing with his paper mills.*

Many, many, good people have been destroyed by his actions. THC is actually still BAD in many places. The fact that it's illegal anywhere, right now, much less, Bad, shows the absolute underbelly of humanity. Thank you, California and Oregon. Thank you, Joe Rogan.

Sure, THC can be an intoxicant, but an open and honest discussion justifying cannabis prohibition fails miserably on any objective basis. It is not even close to as destructive as alcohol and has far more significant benefits. The statistics on the paybacks of Cannabis are compelling. I was always for medical cannabis, but I was unsure of the societal impact of full legalization, alcohol aside. Mike Tyson's recent appearance on the Joe Rogan Experience podcast put that to bed.

I wear a THC patch. That's right. A Patch. I can't even get them where I live now. I have been using two different versions from Surterra Wellness and Alt-Med (Muv) that I legally purchased in Florida. In the United States of America, where I am clearly endowed by my creator with the right to the pursuit of happiness, I cannot legally purchase or use a medication that eliminates constant, nagging, depressive thoughts, because I committed the unspeakable crime of MOVING A COUPLE STATES AWAY. I don't blame 70-year-old ignorance, though that's on the nose. Nope. I blame Washington, DC. I blame our federal legislators. This situation is untenable, and ducking the issue is cowardly. On this issue, more than any other, any true leader should stand up and shape opinion. Any politician that has accepted money from the alcohol lobby, the insurance lobby, or the pharmaceutical lobby, and is not currently doing everything they can to say, "Sorry we fucked you over for no good reason." Should be removed from office… Perhaps, that was still too much Jessica, but it is honest and FACTUALLY CORRECT.

Cannabis WAS used in the practice of early Abrahamic religions. It was the main ingredient in the holy anointing oil used by the priests of Aaron. Any argument against that is either fabricated or mistaken. I really hope religion gets more fun… again!

This is a collage I made as a sort of healing sigil. It's similar to some of my art but less visually appealing. I think you'll get the point.

Notice the word TUAOI in the middle. It's pronounced two owie (like wowie). According to Edgar Cayce, the Tuaoi stone was a stone, used by priests of Atlantis, that was able to transmute negative energy. I am in the camp that believes it is/was an aqua colored stone called Larimar.

I really hope the cannabis rant was not terribly offensive for *most of you*.

"Chuckling?"

Mmmm Hm

I didn't say, "I hope you're not offended," because I think anyone still reading is incapable of understanding the points I made in this chapter. Not at all. In a woo-free sense, many people have a sort of governor on, psychologically. Their minds simply WILL NOT let in ANY INFORMATION that triggers conditioned reactions, driven by survival-based fears.

This is an image I found in the void that captures the essence of this man's legacy.

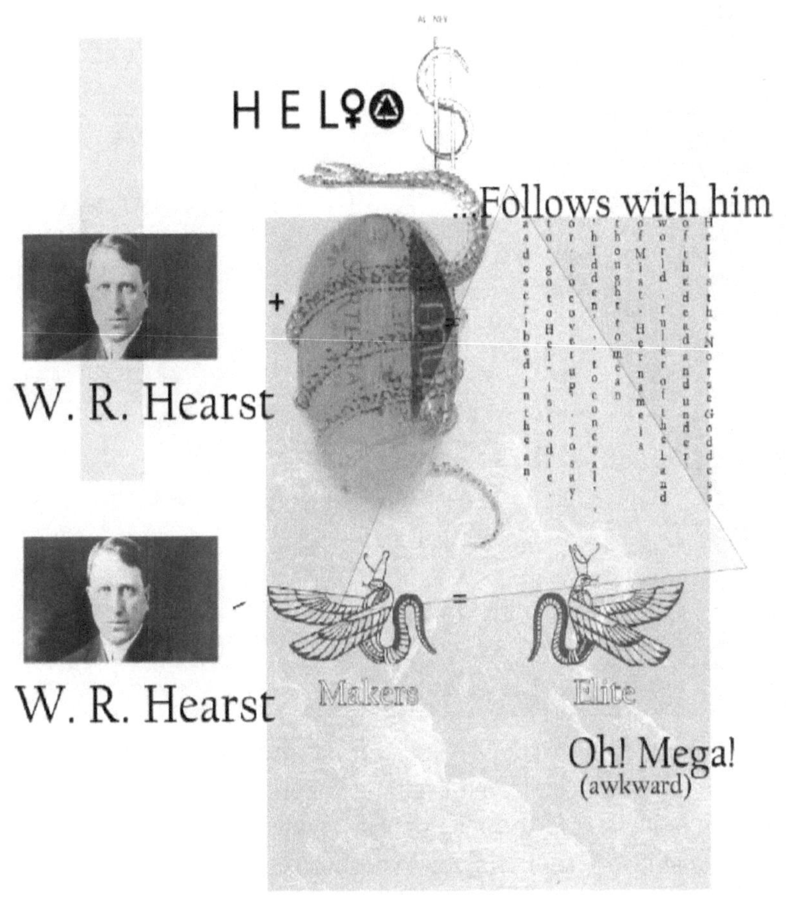

Facing The Sun, They Saw No Shadows

I may have hinted at this… The last year has, from an outside perspective, been difficult. Though I haven't felt much guilt, shame, or embarrassment in quite a while, the world has not stopped. "What is" has been explaining itself to me. Remember when I told you I see more injustice, not less?

Well, some of that was up close. Metaphorically, I've been run over by two companies simply because they perceived that doing so was to their *slight* benefit at the time. Their actions derailed my (other) career and my ability to stay afloat financially. Here's what I noticed through all of it…

The strong are predatory on the weak. Not all of them, but WAY, WAY TOO MANY UPSTANDING MEMBERS OF SOCIETY, RATIONALIZE THE SHIT OUT OF THEIR SELFISH DRIVES. I'm optimistic about the future because I think enough people *can snap out of it* to adjust our heading in time. I understand the rage we see on the left in this country much better than I used to, but the solution starts with seeking to understand all perspectives and devise wise, sustainable win-win-win outcomes that we can all live with. We're stuck in old, binary thinking patterns. As you begin to become more and more conscious, the meaning of that will become very, very clear to you. It'll hit you with the speed and power of a Sammy Sosa home run baseball bat swing in the steroid era.

The critics of postmodernism have some valid points. You can't say that all perspectives are legitimate *and* all truths are relative, while at the same time intentionally implying that your opinion is meta and your ideas infallible.

The current left wing in the united states has *accurately* pointed out that A LOT of our made-up standards of propriety are rooted in arrogance and prejudice. They are right NOT TO ACCEPT the status quo in MANY AREAS.

If you don't think privilege exists, try this experiment. Use a fast-food drive-thru in an old, dirty car. Take it a step further… go through a busy two-lane drive-thru a couple days in a row. I want to see your face when the Mercedes edges in front of you, even though their food won't be ready, because… why?

A Tesla could magically arrive in my driveway. I'll still keep my awesome, fun, '08 RDX. It's in rough shape, but I cherish it.

> "That doesn't sound very hygienic."

> Ha! I'm not glorifying mess but don't underestimate the perspective you can see when someone who was your long lost romance in a jewelry store, and judged you worthy of admittance, shows confusion and even embarrassment when they see you in your car. You don't get to experience that side of people in a newer luxury car. You just don't.

I remember a scene from The West Wing when Cliff Calley's character facetiously explains that he is a Republican because he thinks poor people are gross. Now, Aaron Sorkin creates some of the smartest, good-hearted characters that have ever existed. He's in a class by himself. Of course, it was well understood that Cliff didn't mean what he said in that instance. The problem is… Cliff's comments DO describe a small segment of the Republican Party, whether they are conscious of it or not. To be fair, I said, "small." When evolved people take similar positions FOR VERY DIFFERENT REASONS, people lump both groups together. This is referred to as a pre-trans fallacy.

Now, you might have inferred from those statements that I am a conservative. If you did, you'd be very right and very wrong.

"You just couldn't help yourself there, huh?"

Nope.

Despite the 4 webbed toes that my mom said made me swim faster, I used to be the pride of the family. I had a very bright future. When I was admitted to college, the college I went to was ranked 5th or 6th on several lists of the best colleges in America. I once gave a girlfriend what I would now describe as a "pre-rational" answer to a similar question. It was a regurgitated, conditioned response. I swear I could actually see her losing respect for me. Never again.

I didn't choose this sort of, well, anonymous partnership because the pen name was funny, though it is… at least a little. I considered this carefully, from as many perspectives as I was able. If you read this entire book….

"…and read your blog?"

That *would* help.

…within a year or two, you'll find out just how many views it is possible to take, and it will blow your mind. That is also a promise.

The way I feel about my decision is nuanced. On the one hand, I want to be present in any discussion that may result from this to help us come together if I can. On the other hand, I like my freedom. If you care,

"Hey!"

…another way I could see this going and, again, "Please baby Jesus in a tuxedo shirt," if this book is a financial success. I don't want to be rich, but right now, I couldn't afford a lawyer if I needed one. I'm pricing this at $2.99 because I desperately want to help

"You're laughing again, aren't you?"

You know it, sister.

If you enjoy this book, I will be incredibly joyful, and I promise I won't give two shits as to how you found it.

It is for that reason that the body, *at a much lower volume and more politely than ever* asks, "What is the point of striving to change when we have joy?"

Indeed… and this is an excellent opportunity to increase my credibility.

"Your credibility? Isn't that ego?"

Nope.

THE ONLY reason that increasing the level of credibility that you perceive is desired, which is what I was referring to, is because *it will help you hear me.* Hearing me is a good thing. I already know I'm credible. (light chuckle)

By starting here, and by here, I mean by answering the question, "Why screw with joy?" I can indirectly prove some other claims while teaching you a valuable tool. When *conditioned thoughts* of action, or emotional *reactions*, do not reflect what you consciously believe, there is a disconnect between what you consciously think and what *your body* "thinks." Negative emotions are of the body. Selfish thoughts are of the body. If you have a lot of them, you might be a redneck. Sorry. With so many if-then statements, I had to do it once.

"Yeah, yeah… I have negative emotions AND selfish thoughts. Is my body controlling me, big shot?"

Small shot. Ssmalll shotteh… and how would I know?

I like your enthusiasm, and I understand why you asked, but I'm going to finish my first point, then we'll do the freaky runaway body thing, and then I'm going to finish the not the body thing. At least most of it.

Back to the indirect philosophy proof… If I were acting out of my *old* self(body), I wouldn't risk losing a state like that. I would *joy ride.* It's not even a big decision in that case. However, I'm not.

"Why did you emphasize *old?*

Because what I did worked, and constant observation and prayer seem to have rewired a lot of my old beliefs. We work together now in a much more harmonious fashion. When the body stopped butting in to tell me I couldn't do things and I wasn't worthy, we started getting along.

I am locked in in one direction. I create because I love this big beautiful world and all of the awesome people in it. Any worldly pleasure that I get to experience is a bonus, including physical sensation and positive emotion. I enjoy it while it's here, but it does not affect my desire. THERE'S NOTHING WRONG WITH ENJOYING A BENEFIT WHEN YOU'RE DOING WHAT YOU KNOW IS RIGHT. When you notice thoughts to the contrary, do what I did. As long as I wasn't in a place where it would be observed, I would actually yell "BULLSHIT!!!" "Completely made up!"

What I desire above all else is to help and to heal with beauty, art, and wisdom. It is my sincere wish that this short book does some of that.

Now, to estimate a generic answer to your question…

Yep. You are WAY in the background. You get to drive about 15% of the time.

> "There is absolutely zero chance that is true."

> How do you really feel?

>> It is true. Don't take my word for it... look it up. A fun way to verify would be to watch a "Talk at Google," given by Brian Greene, the author of 48 Laws of Power.

Runaway body, for sure. (chuckles at the thought of you chasing your body) It is, but don't take my word for it. Learn to become still (meditate) and watch your thoughts. Watch your actions also. All of them. Here are two pieces that I made to illustrate this point. A more visually appealing version of Spooky Action has been done as a collaboration, by Thomas Bell. Thomas has a gallery in Asheville, NC, and his masterful paintings can also be found at www.thomasbellart.com.

SPOOKY ACTION (Below)

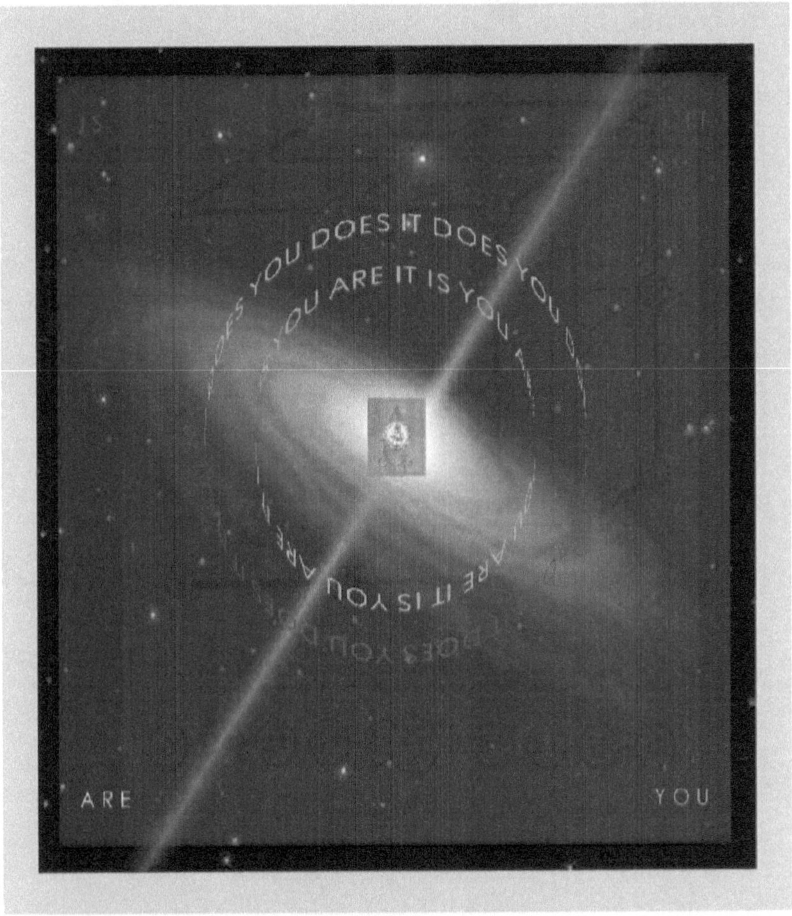

INFINITE MERGE(Below)

In tiny writing, the phrases, "If God, then Us." And "If Us, then God" are used. The image appearing in 3D actually has one side and one edge. Trace it. Adding color would've confused the point.

Mass De-Wooing

At this point, if I don't clarify the whole you/you/Self/self/body thing, I could lose you for good, so that's where we're going next. We're going deep.

DON'T ASK YOUR BODY IF IT WANTS THC!

"What? Why not?"

I was totally fucking with you. Yes! THC! Now! Not too much, though, and get as still as you possibly can before you partake in the sacrament.

"You can't be serious."

Definitely not serious, but I am sincere.

"Ok… not the body?"

Thanks. I get distracted sometimes. We have arrived at this moment simultaneously way too early, and without a moment to spare, so let the mind fuck begin.

"There you go again! That's unintelligible."

Oh, ok.

This is going to take focus, and while you probably have a little more than you did 10 pages ago, you may not have much to spare. This is important. It is deep and steep, and it has the potential to seriously piss you off if you are at a low level of consciousness.

"That was sneaky."

What part of "mind-fuck" didn't you understand?

"Uhh, the intensity?"

I would have liked to teach you some more straightforward stuff first. However, a lot of what I would consider reachable, while light and fluffy to me, could very well mean death by 1,000 semantic cuts for you.

If I don't first give you a rough outline of this concept, it could be tough to understand.

"What?"

Call it what you will… misidentification, miscommunication. I would miss you either way. (chuckle) Did I mention THC?

Here's what it boils down to… You have all sorts of programs installed on that thing that need to go. To make sure you understand the words that are coming out of my (pineal gland?). Again, **you have installed *MANY* subconscious applications** throughout your life, the majority during adolescence, that generate conditioned, reactive thoughts. If you watch a spontaneous argument closely, you can see pre-packaged, automatic responses flying back and forth like ping-pong balls.

Here's an example: Right around the time that you discovered games, something else happened…

Picture a child. 18-24 Months is my best guess. The child is smiling. His/Her loving caregiver is smiling. Since the child has, up to this point, only identified as a "we," I will refer to the parent as "Big we," and the child as "Little we."

"Big we" has some keys…

"Big we" gives we the keys to "Little we."

"Little we" smiles.

Next, "Little we" hand the keys to "Big we."

Right around that moment, it happened… Life enjoying itself became reciprocity. It was one of the very first things each of us made up... the arbitrary partition between self and other, based on confusing rapid changes in density with actual separation. At first, it was an idea, or perhaps a new perspective. Neither of us was there, so it's hard to know for sure.

Yes, I am chuckling.

"Are you in my head?"

Yep. Jumped in for a minute to help steer. Just go with it. Just for a little while. Had to lock you in a little deeper before I asked you to work at the flea market. (chuckle)

But seriously… This request is not rooted in arrogance. It comes from a place of compassion. Please do not stop reading until you feel like you are at least beginning to understand each of the next two concepts. You can pause at the end of this chapter, then again on page 47, if you would like. Both of these concepts were difficult for me to "get."

I want to show you a piece of Art that I created to visually represent the danger that waking up without a guide presents. Now, for you perfectionists and Art snobs… I lost the file before I could clean it up thoroughly, but I think it communicates what I wanted it to. I am 41; the title is *A Pirate Looks at 42.*

I sincerely believe it is by the grace of God and his/her/zer design for evolution that I am not sitting in a mental hospital. It was touch and go for a while. I have been in the process of waking up for over a year, and I have been close to madness a few times. It feels to me as if, as a species, we are on the edge of a breakthrough. I hope that means there are a lot of people

Not the Body – Finally Explained

I hope you ate your Wheaties. We're going to rip the Band-Aid off pretty fast.

Ok, so what I refer to as "the body" is "your body," which initially identified as a WE before it created YOU *as a thought form*.

Thoughts are energy, even from the perspective of materialism. This is one place where science and ancient wisdom converge.

Light is also energy, so there is a link between the physical body and anything in your field of vision that can transmit information. Think fiber optics on a micro scale. If it were not so, you could not be aware of it.

> "Whoah! I'm starting to see it… Can I identify as a group and an individual at the same time?"

> Congratulations. I'll answer that question at the end of the third book.

> "Bogus."

Why?

> "If you make us wait until the end of the book…"

> Didn't act on it, but I saw what you're referring to arise as a possibility. Saw it clear as day. If I hold that nugget for the end of the book, I can manipulate some people into finishing it. Just like that? Is that what you mean?

> "Then how is that not a lie? It seems at least a little dishonest."

NOISE!!!!! STATIC!!!!! NOT REAL!!!!! NONE OF IT!!!!!
COMPLETELY   MADE   UP!!!!

 The choice had already happened, based entirely on these two facts:

1)It will take more groundwork. A lot more.

2) After pointing you in the direction where you will be able to begin waking up, it's a very close second, regarding the intangible value of this project.

Now, because IT identified as WE or US wholly and first, IT had to disassociate WE from I.

Here's a fun aside. Identical twins separate first as a thought form they call "you," when referring to themselves or the other, but what they mean is "us."

<u>"Is that why they seem to be connected?"</u>

Perhaps.

How easy is it for you to entirely shift your identity? Not very, right? I have read some scary stuff that alludes to the fact that it can be done by force… but that doesn't seem wise to me. We're not going anywhere near *those* woods.

NOW, let's really get after it. Open up your toolbox.

About where we left off on how YOU will REALIZE (To Make Real) that you are not your body. You see, your body *was you* before it thought you up as a cloud of mental energy called "I," and the electron that called itself "WE," but meant "US," or "I" jumped from that toddler body into the "I" that "WE" (you) created and then promptly changed its name to "I."

<u>"…and then?"</u>

Then, they fell asleep. Wasn't that fun?

<u>"I was joking. No. Give me a minute."</u>

<u>"Ok, so I had to read that about eight times, but I think I'm starting to understand. Had a question… It was… Oh! What's the physical location of the created "I" that the "we" electron… uh… jumped to… and…?</u>

Changed its name to "I?"

<u>"Yes."</u>

By George, I think you've got it!

<u>"So, this is not only LIKE electricity. It actually IS electricity?"</u>

Ever worn leather soled shoes on new carpet? All those electrons jumped INTO the carpet in transit. The tight friction on a bumpy road attracted them. Your leather soles allowed them to jump into you. Literally, right into "you."

You can stop reading for now if you would like. We're on steadier ground.

Here's something fun to fill the rest of the blank page. His name is
Pomegranate Helper. When I started this, I had no idea he was in there.

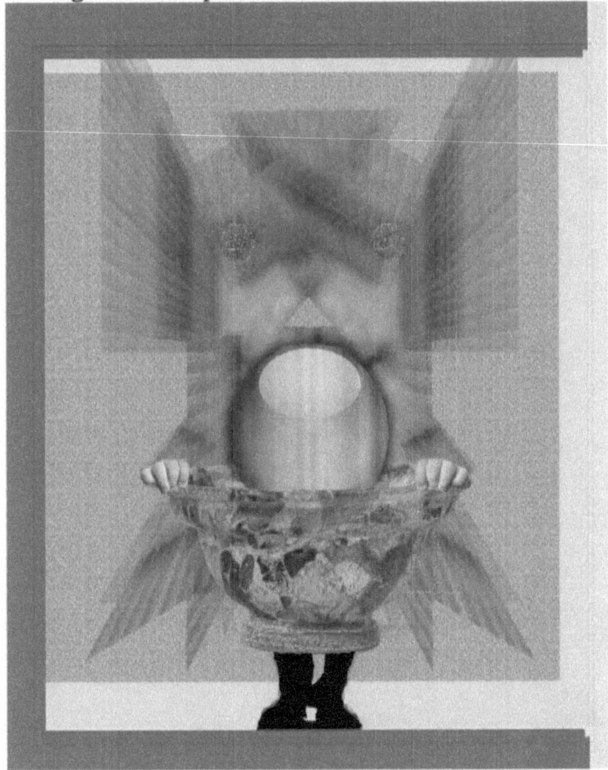

The On-Ramp

When watching our thoughts and our actions, we pay careful attention to
what would best be described as a *reaction* (as opposed to a response).
Responses are blends of Self and self. Reactive responses are self(body).
When you spot a negative emotion OR a selfish thought (just the extremes, at
first), ask your body/ego the following questions:

    1) What would it feel like if I knew why:
       a) I reacted that way?

b) I had that thought?

Shut up and let it answer. Get as still as you possibly can and relax. This is a MUCH easier skill than learning to rid the mind of all conditioned thinking. Your higher self can quickly shut up. Mainly because, starting out, the body is loud. It's arrogant, forceful, and easy to hear. It wants to brag about how it "helps you." Right now, we're gathering information, nothing more. Next question:

> 2) Is there any experience from my childhood that may have contributed to installing that belief? If so, what did it feel like?
> 3) What would it feel like if I remembered my mother's beliefs and attitudes related to _________? Be specific.
> 4) What would it feel like if I remembered my father's beliefs and attitudes related to _________?

That's how I started. Every time I was disturbed, *in any way*, I would *interrogate the body*.

Do you now, or at any time in the future, want to think of yourself less than you do now? It is possible. It should be relatively easy to believe that it, but belief is not enough. We must grab truth where we find it and apply logic to build to a stronger truth claim.

Now, *we could* argue for a while about whether we can validate the following statement, *"If it is possible to think of myself less than I do now, then it is possible to think of myself not at all."*

Luckily, that won't be necessary. This one works and can't be denied: *"If it is possible to think of myself less than I do now, then it is possible, with action, to think of myself much, much less than I do now."*

That's one way that real knowledge, which is different than information, can shift our perspective. There's no way out of it. If a universal conditional (if/then) statement is a true statement, and the hypothesis is correct, then the conclusion is also right. Always.

This process can get off track quickly in several ways. A few tips:

> 1) Do not ask the body if something is real. Not now, anyway. When you can consciously access the body, you can completely realign the body's BS (chuckle) meaning belief structure, and work WITH

it.

2) Righteous anger can be pure masculine love when it is in defense of something larger than "I," and it is needed.

"BULL SHIT!!!! CALLING BULLSHIT!!!!   BOTH!!!! TWO BULLSHITS!!!!"

Cite your source.

"On the second one THAT WOULD BE Turn the other cheek! Everyone knows non-violence is better!"

It is. Never said otherwise.

"But you said…"

I said when needed. When required.

Justified anger is required when the people you are trying to help can't be reached any other way. Violence is the right action in defense of virtue when all else fails or is sure to fail. Period.

"You mean like honor killings?"

NO! No. I don't mean like honor killings but keep thinking like that.

"Getting weird again."

You *are* an expert... Why?

"Because I think you said terrorist shit. That's why."

Now's a good time to address *possible erroneous conclusions you might think up and blame on me.* It is theoretically possible that at least one of them will be so incredibly wrong, it may seem like a reversal of reality.

If the conclusion, attributed to me, is far off course, your body will force-feed you a smorgasbord of judgment. Watch for that. Before you unconsciously follow, please ask yourself, "Is it possible that I misunderstood what the author meant?" It's not only possible. It's highly likely. Why?

For starters, we are going off of the map! Many of you may be in unfamiliar territory much of the time. If you are still with me, you have A REAL SHOT to radically evolve. I'm not guessing, either. I have a logical justification.

I would much prefer that didn't happen. It doesn't always have to, but If you (referring to a blend this time) do not trust me, you could choose to abandon our carriage ride deep in the woods. No Bueno. Ooh… If it helps you, I'm good with being a horse. Seriously. That should be a little more proof that my goal is to help you, not to control you.

I Think I Can, But WE May Need Help

Picture this… You are vacationing on a lake. A diamond sparkling lake… and in the light of the full moon, one of the human beings you love most in this world sleepwalks out to the end of the dock. You can see them from the window of your warm cottage as they cross the half-way point, on their way to a *predator-filled* lake. If you are a parent, picture your child *as a child, walking quickly into danger*.

Question: What would you do? If you answered, scream like hell and run like hell or something close to that, here's my follow up:

Would that look like love?

Did it when Jesus Christ scolded the money changers in the temple? Why not turn the other cheek then?

The title of this book could have been The Good News.

"Why?"

Because I think it is good news.

I would love to work it out with some smart people, but the best as I can figure it… I think I am supposed to be some sort of John the Baptist for this age.

I understand God differently, but I absolutely know that what Jesus was describing is just as available today as it was then.

The entire Bible makes a whole lot more sense, now.

Why Have I…?

In my experience, If I cannot create a rational model to integrate new truth with consensus reality, or at least a modified version thereof, I can't remember it, much less explain it.

As soon as the monkey mind saw a squirrel, figuratively, it would take off. For many, many years, aha moments were fleeting. They were always joyful experiences, but I could never hold on to them. I suppose I hoped that having spiritual experiences would still help me evolve, even though I was *unable* to remain conscious of their essence.

As you awaken, you will encounter "Who the hell does this girl/guy think he is?" Sadly, it is the most common conditioned reaction of the conditioned mind. It's woven into the fabric of our misunderstanding. It even has a name. I am referring to the *tall poppy syndrome.* That's not arrogance. It's not hubris. For all of our sakes, I wish it were.

Most human beings see life from a zero-sum perspective. That means we accept the following belief, which we deduced in pre-school, to be true: "IF he/she/ze succeeds, there is less potential for success available to me." Sound familiar? It seems rational enough. I will tell you in no uncertain terms… that belief is categorically false. It sure can seem real though, can't it? It did to me for 41 years.

You see, our toolbox is virtually filled with false knowledge, which some of you may be tempted to see as a bad thing. It's not. It is indescribably wonderful. However, since I am all too aware of the upper limits of shifts in human perceptions, I will only ask you to consider and change if you wish, one belief at a time. To experience this book harmoniously, the idea that much of what we believe is incorrect must be entertained. It's too much to expect, but it's not too much to ask.

Now, I told you I would give you clear reasons for each deduction, and I will honor that, but as loosening your grip on false beliefs is crucial, I can't bloody well accomplish in a few paragraphs what I envision to be the main object of this book. To be fair, you need only crack the door open. All that is required is that you be *willing* to believe that *some* of what you know for sure *may not be true.*

I sincerely hope that a wide variety of people will read this book. To those of you with an appreciation for novelty… from the perspective of consensus reality, I am bona fide in a few things: Bi-Polar type 1 and the Math I learned through high-school among them. In the interest of transparency, I learned A LOT of math through my junior year of high school. I discovered it a) while I loved it and b) before I started drinking, I remember more than I have forgotten, even though it was 25 years ago.

Again, do not let what anyone else says, "Cannot be" distract when searching for *what is.* Find out for yourself what is true. Follow these guys' example:

Sean Carroll & Richard Feynman – nerd humor

Dreams

I dream about auditing a few of the classes I rarely attended, and barely passed in college, but I dream of doing that now, not then. Paradoxically, if I could go back in time, I wouldn't change a thing. Not a thing. Why? Because both my desire and my ability to create beauty and harmony were forged in fire. If I had not been so wrong, for so long, I might not be able to see clearly today.

Regrets are utterly worthless. They are pins holding down a false understanding to justify their own existence. They exist ONLY from a self-centered perspective. Day after day, right action after right action, approaching life from a sincere desire to help others, all regrets fall away. For that matter, so do self-centered fears.

When I am disturbed in any way, the problem is my perspective. Please do not take that to mean that error and injustice don't exist. I see more error and wrong, not less, but I am better able to contemplate solutions from a peaceful place of radical acceptance. It is rarely the case that things don't "go my way."

No woo-peddling there. I don't have a wand, and I don't create all of reality as I go along. The answer is simple and much more beautiful. I rarely have a way.

I Am That I Am

Drop the blow torch, oh powerful destroyer of poppies. The title, in this instance, is simply meant to *describe* what we have traditionally referred to as God.

> "What we have referred to? Do you believe in God?"

> I could say yes. I could say… maybe. Both would be partially true, and entirely irrelevant?

> "Again. Huh?"

I could answer based on either a) consensus understanding of God or b) my experience. I believe in the God I have experienced, which may or may not resemble convention.

"Explain."

Here goes.

If reality consistently arises contrary to any aspect of your belief system… you can safely cast the erroneous belief aside… for now. What do you mean FOR NOW? God doesn't change. Agreed, but irrelevant. The rules of emerging reality can and does change, and that does not have to be attributed to a change in God. God doesn't change… but his/her messages of guidance delivered through the best of US absolutely do.

It is precisely for this reason that we should not interpret ancient scriptures, based on what they mean NOW. A wiser perspective is to look at them considering what they said when they were written and not a penny more. For that matter, not a penny less, either.

Consider the following example… "The Bible says, Adam and Eve, not Adam and Steve." I shit you not: that came out of a preacher (that I provoked) less than two months ago…yep…prejudice and ignorance are alive and well in 2019. Because of the path of division that we accept, I was on the phone with… forgive me if I don't get the phrasing precisely correct, but I believe he described himself as either the outreach leader or compassion minister. While neither of those titles is even remotely accurate, that's more or less how he referred to himself. This wasn't a dying church, either, which can be translated as… it was a mega-church, complete with preaching holograms and ridiculous, condescending replicas of Harry Potter crests.

He had reached out to me after I responded to an email I received, thanking me for my contribution last year. When I had a job, I tithed 10%. I even tithed $1000 when I sold a possession for $10,000 last fall, though I was unemployed. Look at that! I knew it. Shameless virtue signaling! Slow your roll, Poppy. I would rather stay anonymous for now, remember. Besides, it took every bit of that good intent to quiet the monkey mind, so you bet your ass I include it.

Now for the fun part of the conversation. This guy was very proud of how many gay people attended his church. His exact words were, "It's not discrimination that they can't hold positions of leadership. You see because no unmarried congregant that's living in sin could hold a position of leadership either." Rrrright… still moronic, but not the same thing. I pointed that out to him and told him in no uncertain terms that he was not following the example of Jesus. So what? I know Buddha too. Though… I am closest to the smiling fat version. Big lesson there. Anyway, "No, you are not, sir!" really got him going. He actually hung up on me. No kidding. I guess he didn't like my answer to his question. He asked, indignantly, "IF I am not following the example of Jesus Christ, why, THEN, do we have so many gay people that attend our church?" To which, I calmly replied, "That's an easy one. You're the best of bad options. You have great music and a relaxed dress code." That was when he so eloquently used his Adam and Steve rebuttal. I suppose, "Because you ate all the other churches," would've also worked, but I think he would have been even more unwilling to accept that.

Given that they have served their clearly utilitarian purpose, which *was* to enable the core teachings to spread across continents and millennia without the aid of anything even remotely resembling the technology we currently possess, why then do we still assume the parts of ancient, sacred texts that relate to strict transference are valid. You know… nothing shall be added or taken away? Still? Why? Remember, there was no printing press present at the council of Nicaea. Just a bunch of bishops that were already a pale reflection of their counterparts from a few centuries earlier. If the message changes because we change, shouldn't any possibility, however unlikely it may seem, be judged by modern standards? No? Please review the following statistics and answer again. Community churches without electrified boogie bands are dropping like flies. This chart contains data from a study I found called, "America, the Diverse" Their graph is more apparent, and prettier for that matter. Feel free to google it.

Religious Affiliation by Age Group

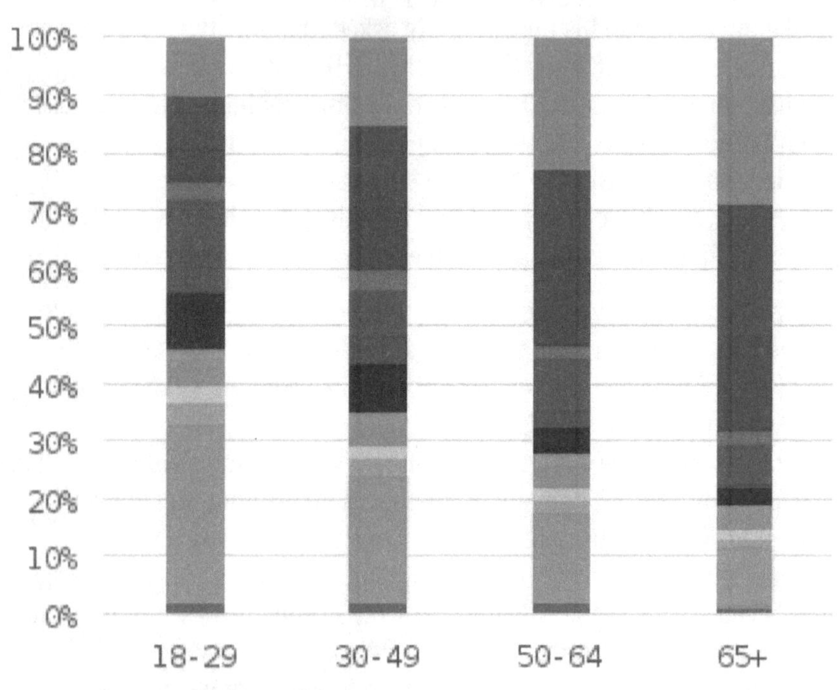

<u>"Why is the trend line so drastic?"</u>

Good observation. Those are some very steep increases among the unaffiliated, and some steep drops among the most significant affiliations.

I can think of a few reasons…

Again… Adam and Steve? Really? Still? There are arguments against that in most of our families, and they are plain as day. They ARE. Yeah…but what about Leviticus? That's one of the oldest books in the Old Testament/Torah. Answer this honestly… Is stoning the adulterers in your tribe still OK? I am not asking if you think adultery is a good idea. It's always a rotten, cowardly thing to do, but death by stoning? At this point, does the punishment still fit the crime? Did it ever? It is my honest opinion that it did indeed. When that was written down, we were living in small tribes. When you lived with ten families, and two families were torn apart, the survival or the tribe was in grave peril. You see, merely being willing to look at scripture evenly, through a lens from the past AND allow for the possibility that some passages should be studied, but discounted, considering our present circumstance. Not only does that perspective move us forward. It also helps us understand from whence we came. The bathwater is old and smelly. The babies that it benefitted are long gone.

Still not convinced… Christian, Buddhist, Muslim, and Hindu monasteries all held slaves. In the Commentarii De Beatis Orientalibus, written by the missionary John of Ephesus (507–589 AD), John tells us that monks and monasteries are allowed to own slaves, but not in large numbers, and not for the same purposes as the rich, who are criticized for their *style* of slaveholding. Now, many monks and monasteries freed their slaves… eventually. Still clinging, huh? It was too long ago? Really? Have you read Ephesians 6:5? To refresh your memory, this is the New Living Translation: "Slaves, obey your earthly masters with deep respect and fear. Serve them sincerely as you would serve Christ." Do we still need that? For you fundamentalist, last gaspers, I have two words for you. Slave Bibles. You know, if you fight hard enough for your limitations, you do get to keep them. That can be attributed to smiling fat Buddha or baby Jesus in a tuxedo shirt. Look at that… after all of these years… the donkey and the tram are the same price. That obscure and challenging to follow reference was brought to you via my memory of one of Ron White's legendary stand-up routines, In which he points out some humorous occurrences on vacation to Grand Canyon.

For the Love of God, Think for Yourself

That isn't self-pity. Woe is not me. I am merely describing "What is" based on my own observations. Social proof has always been one of the most potent influence methods. The *need* for social proof, as a prerequisite to action, is well past "unhealthy."

You should be able to see evidence of that from your own experience. Thanks, middle school. Thanks, FaceBook. That instinct, or body belief, is based on an erroneous assumption. I would love to have two wise people with different backgrounds both tell you to read this. Who knows… Maybe someday there will be. It would be great if this became an overnight success story, but I don't expect it.

My "story" doesn't matter in the least to me, except where I can practically retrace my steps to help you. If I give you the cliff notes version, you should be able to understand how I got here, but for your sake, I hope you find a more natural way. There's really nothing that can make assumptions that we've held all our lives pliable, so much a series of betrayals, experienced while holding a virtuous intention, and taking moral action. Not only did I see where my assumptions had been wrong from my perspective, but I was also forced to reconcile a seeming contradiction. Activities that I saw as diabolically evil came from people that didn't have horns. Most of them even had children.

I was forced to see that our thoughts and corresponding actions arise from several very different sources, and somehow, we identify as all of them. Why? We have never even been willing to *consider the possibility* that we are wrong at a fundamental level. It's painful! Duh! At first, anyway.

I have evolved, and that word was chosen carefully. I not only have a willingness to question my own BS (belief structure), I am genuinely excited when I find an error in MY BS. Under certain conditions, I can tap an inner resource that allows me to reprogram my body. I am going to tell you what those conditions are, but for those of you not living on the west coast, it may come as a shock.

How do I *have* conflicting thoughts? How do I resolve them? I will answer both questions, but first, I humbly request that we do a little mind hack together: If you read this to learn something that you can use to help *all of life*, you can retain *nearly all of it* that you choose to.

That's exciting, right? That's the least outrageous of my claims, and I am positive that it's true. It's not as easy as it sounds, but if you approach anything you do with that intention, you will not experience self-centered fear, and focus will come quickly. More importantly, you will also notice that concerns related to group identification, based on territorial instincts, will become exceedingly rare.

Please don't believe ANYTHING without close examination and careful testing. Not what you read, and until you absolutely know you have a robust and stable connection to spirit, don't believe much of what you think or feel, either.

This is called Humane Lies. It's an anagram for Enuma Elish, the Sumerian/Akkadian creation myth. I thought that was interesting. You'll get a lot more examples of using phoenix translations as mental crowbars. Our myths are Humane Lies, aren't they?

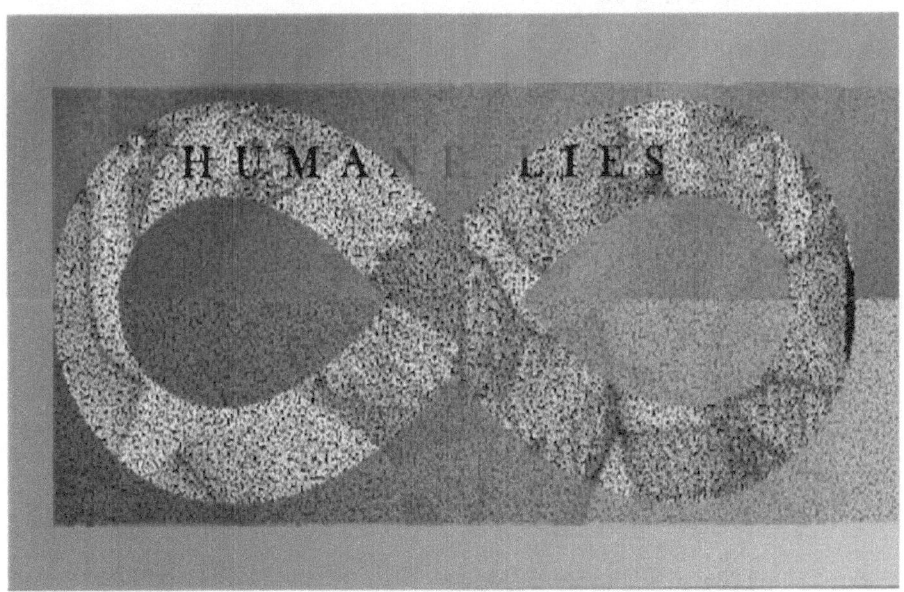

Put Me In, Coach!

A little while ago, I took a personality profile. I am an SIDC, which means, in descending order, I possess steadiness, then the ability to influence, then the ability to be direct and decisive. Last, and certainly least, I am compliant. The nickname for that profile is apparently, "The Coach." That means I am much more STEADY than COMPLIANT.

"How can that possibly be?"

It's quite simple.

When the veil drops and the monkey mind shuts up, our problems are solvable, but we are often comically looking for the solutions in the wrong direction. If we would only allow ourselves to turn around and look, the truth would be staring right at us, undeniably, plainly, waiting to be discovered.

Please take a moment to ponder the following question: Why don't we look? The answer is beautifully hopeful. It comes in two parts: First, I swear to anything and everything holy that the world is sleepwalking. That's right, most of you are stuck in conditioned, reactive thought about 85% of the time. You are involved in a series of reactions that you see as your choices, which really aren't. Am I saying that there is no such thing as free will? Not exactly but I am saying there's little free will on a water slide.

It's going to be OK. There's certainly no reason for panic. However… our collective beliefs, also known as "consensus reality," are wrong **most of the time**. Picture this: a house of cards floating on an increasingly unstable, soaking wet piece of cardboard, resting upon a densely fogged lake so still that the entire surface is mirrored. Sit with that. Hold it loosely.

"If that visual is much more akin to *what actually is* than say, the nightly news, why does the news *feel* so real?"

First, it doesn't at all seem real to me. Hidden motives are in bright flashing lights. Questions from either side of both right and left leaning discussion shows are slanted. Sometimes they know it. Often, they don't.

"Their questions are slanted, and they *don't know*?"

When Siddhartha Gautama said, "I am awake," I think ONE thing he meant was, "I no longer react with conditioned responses and believe I am the doer. On the contrary, I respond with the help of God."

Let's try a few mental exercises together, shall we?   The next few chapters should really gel for you at this point.

Where Should We Start?

What's the first thing you would like to ponder?

"<u>Does God exist?</u>"

That's actually a great example, but you don't want to hear any more shit about

Now… Imagine you just asked the Cheshire cat the same question.

I started writing this in response to a question. I thought others might enjoy it. The tone of this is light, but the subject is profound. I do not intend to mock.

Is an apple aware of the apple tree? The orchard? Would an apple have any idea of the tree's intent or purpose? If you have never seen a tree, but you have seen a green apple, would you assume a tree exists? An orchard? A continent? A Planet Earth?

 At the request of the quotation mark conservation society, please take note of the following disclaimer: Using planet as a verb is the least offensive grammatical or punctuation liberty taken in this article. The reader may experience a sharp increase in wisdom at the expense of a slight regression in give-a-shit. The overall punctuation league has publicly declared that they have lost faith in the existence of Microsoft.

1) SOMETHING creates the big bang.

2) A big hot mound of prickles and goo starts expanding

3) "It" begins to star and galaxy.

4) Some of the stars start to planet.

5) Some faceless planets do some gas-ing, a little watering, then some landing.

6) Then comes life-ing. Pretty soon, life-ing gets to algae-ing.

7) After that, mossing and leaving.

8)Perhaps some insect-ing, a little flowering.

9) Now, it's time for the real fun to begin… it starts lizard-ing and fishing.

10) Some of the fishing and some of the lizard-ing turns into birding.

11) Sometimes there's shrewing that turns into aping, and then aping (or occasionally lizard-ing?) turns into bipedal smarting. On some planets, they call that peopling.

12) Bipedal smarting gets dicey. It has to go *just right* to have any chance of starship-ing.

13) If it reaches the starship-ing phase before kaboom-ing, it joins

the intergalactic federation. (or starts one)

Now… back to the apples…Are "you" a tree, a branch, an apple, or an orchard? Mindbender: is your answer people-ist?

Let's say you don't get to choose… You blink into existence from the perspective of an apple seed. You can use only seed senses within the bounds of your seed casing and, perhaps, slightly outside. If another seed "seeded" over to you that there was such thing as a planet and that you were a part of it. Would you, could you confirm or deny his seedy claim? Would you have any evidence?

Back to peopling… Is your lung cell-ing or are you? Perhaps is the more substantial "IT" doing it? Why is it either/or? Is it either/or?

Do "You" do "It," or does "It" do "You?"

I showed you this image earlier. Does it mean more or less after

going through that exercise?

<u>"How About Circumcision?"</u>

Curious thought…   OK, Remember the story of Cain and Abel? To refresh your memory… God did not respect Cain's offering of fruit from the ground.

Let's say you're in caveman land and this whole new sacrifice craze is going around. Think about a caveman who desired something intensely. This guy is dedicated. I mean, he's open-minded, brave (low neuroticism), and THEREFORE highly creative… what might he have thought to try? Well, we know Abraham's ancestors came correct. They tried removing something very dear to them indeed. They sent it up to heaven in clouds of smoke.

<u>"You can't just do that."</u>

Do what?

Regardless of "who's shit" we're talking about, ponder the idea for yourself. I'll grant you; it could be terrible. I have bad ideas all the time. That one could be the worst idea I've had in a while. Guess what? If it is, it is. Low neuroticism plus high openness equals high creativity, not perfection.

However, in this case, there is supporting testimony.

"Is the witness credible?"

Pretty sure he is, yes.

In John 7:22, Jesus Christ states that Moses gave them circumcision, but it came from *his ancestors*. Now, a narrow-minded Christian will most likely feel the urge to correct me here, saying that he was referring to Abraham. Maybe. Maybe not.

Those brave men survived and passed it on. Somehow, thank you doesn't seem appropriate.

"How about the Eucharist?"

I was contemplating that one… You know, for the REALLY LONG TIME WE LIVED IN CLANS, do you think it's possible, a caveman got the idea to eat the chief when he died, to see if he could get his powers/wisdom/who knows? Could someone that ambitious, creative, and brave have STRICTLY AS A CORRELATION often/sometimes become chief? Would he have instructed his son to continue the practice? Forgive the vulgarity, but I have no idea: are some humans safe to eat and some not? Watching the version of the Gospel of John that is in the HEALING tab, I got this strange sensation that Jesus COULD POSSIBLY have been referencing a meme that was present at the time of Jesus. If Jesus SAYS that Abraham taught circumcision, but IT CAME FROM THEIR ANCESTORS. Could this be similar? What if the Spirit DID come into being as a scientific process we don't understand yet relating to electrons, thought waves, orienting… for say… communication? For simplicity's sake, should we call that "the word," or is that blasphemy? No? How about "holy spirit," I mean Jesus truth bombed us with this one (Time-lapse truth bomb):

"It is amazing if it was for the spirit that flesh came into existence. And it is amazing indeed if spirit (came into existence) for the sake of the body. But as for me, I am amazed at how this great wealth has come to dwell in this poverty."

It's actually from the Gospel of Thomas, which was found in a cave in upper Egypt in 1945. There is little doubt surrounding the circumstance. It's well established a group of Coptic monks buried it, among many other codices, after Emperor Constantine converted Rome to Christianity in 326 CE. Now, they hid it to prevent it from being destroyed, so I guess we shouldn't be surprised that the established narrative is for good and faithful Christians to ignore it completely. That's rational. That makes perfect sense…

If you're still reading at this point, you probably know this already, but I was being facetious.

At the Beginning of All That Begatting, Something Begun
(Chapter title is an homage to The West Wing)

Want to hear a hypothetical story of God dunking on humanity right before they took to the stars? Remember the popcorn ball from the 80's classic, *Real Genius?*

I suggest using the *James Earl Jones voice* in your head to narrate.

Nobody believed in me. By their actions, I'd say many that said they did really do not. Just for fun… as a part of my continuously evolving plan, I thought I'd write a modern parable, freestyle.

You'd never believe any human telling the story in this age without a lot of help, that's for sure, so I thought I'd include him in the story, WITHOUT HIS KNOWLEDGE, and then adjust his settings to "Rock the world." Fun, huh? That way, when he realizes what's happened, he'll have A SPORTING CHANCE at communicating the story.

Now, for those of you that had a somewhat more intimate experience on the bus ride to school, please read slowly.

"Hey!"

What? God doesn't do anything half-assed. Neither does James Earl Jones for that matter

I knew that all the kooky holy blood holy grail stories would be recycled into Dan Brown movies right as my demonstration of awe and wonder was getting good, so I started with this:

I chose an honest human and named him _________ Sinclair McSomethingorother. The name will obviously vary slightly to protect the author's (more like cast member's) identity for now, but you get the idea – St. Clair as a middle name with a Scottish last name.

"Got it."

OK!

Now, _________ Sinclair McSomethingorother had at least two sons and gave his second son the middle name, Sinclair. Of course, he was still a McSomethingorother. Now, this honest man with a pretty good life was virtuous *and* intelligent, but he gave me, you know, God, no credit for either. _________ went to Dartmouth in the 1930s and played a varsity sport. He then served in the US Navy during WW2 and had a successful career as a stockbroker. He sure was a swell fella, and at that time that meant something, all on its own.

Two Sinclair McSomethingorothers? Who does that?

This isn't supposed to be me, Cheryl.

Oh…. God, can you answer that? She sounds pissed.

It was intended to be a barely visible flare. I don't do "obvious" often. It actually pisses me off when I have to, so both I, and this guy that I chose, will give you more than enough to confirm, but I was signaling you to WATCH. I'm not saying the story doesn't get much, much harder to dismiss as coincidence, but that's all you get in this book.

The second son's second son also went to Dartmouth, but he dropped out after one year and got married. He and his new bride lived at his parents' lake house.

After that marriage failed…

He went into the Navy, and he married a sweet, tall, brilliant, beautiful southern redhead, who's…

> God/Darth Vader is going to skip over some parts now. If not, this will get way too confusing. I'll fill in the rest of the story in another book.

You'll get a damn coupon.

________ had a Christian religious experience on April 27th of 2018. He had visions of torsion fields, a singularity at heart, and a clear understanding of many things that had baffled him to that point. What happened from there forward *may* shock you. We'll leave every other detail out, but my Tool's ex still works for the company that they both worked for at that time. Before the white light experience, they seemed to be doing much better, but he was married to an atheist. Uh-oh. He decided to divorce her because it was a clear indication that he was dangerous. Good thing THE LEADERSHIP of the privately-owned company are all honest-to-goodness Christians. I mean… having a religious experience in a company full of atheists could have been awful. I remember feeling very grateful that I had avoided such a fate. I enjoyed thanking each of them individually for being good stewards.

I know… what are the odds? Today, it's hard to find a boss that will pray with you and tell you that tithing ten percent is the only thing the Bible says, "Test me" on. It's even harder to find a place where ALL OF THE LEADERSHIP are _strong Christians_.

Even with the divorce and the cosmetic surgeries, he didn't see it coming… He didn't think what happened was even possible. He had not yet seen that they were basically sleepwalking, and in their defense, she probably used a lot of leaven.

That said, I honestly wouldn't be surprised AT ALL to learn that the man listens in on calls of distressed homeowners' pleadings for fun.

Their secret weapon is a revolving financing package with a meager minimum payment, so that their "customers," and I am not referring to end consumers, can tactfully sell the products they manufacture at an exorbitant mark-up.

To my former employer: I have received your threats. I left your name out. I have reported you to the FBI, so you can put a hit on me if you want to, but much, much more will be revealed if you do. Besides, God wrote this chapter, anyway.

He was fired in late August 2018. It was unrelated, I'm sure, but coincidentally, it happened the very next business day after their divorce was final.

> _"Truthful?"_

> Obviously sarcastic.

> _"You must've sucked!"_

> You would think so, wouldn't you?

In a corporate report from March of 2018, a member of the upright Christians brigade wrote in a weekly report that sales were projected to be up 30% from new accounts that had occurred since the previous August. He started work as their sales manager the previous June.

After that, he worked at a resort for 21 days and a restaurant for 11 days.

What a disappointment. Right? I mean… those facts that look pretty damning…

We'll see where your breaking point is, regarding the circumstances of this never-ending unfolding story. There's a reason I don't make things "obvious." You're probably right. I mean, you guys are all watching for 666, aren't you? Why is 666 supposed to be significant? Oh, that's right, because it's an inversion of the holy trinity. I'm number 1. I created you on day six, remember?

I'm going to give you a thought experiment to do on your own…

This is a passage from the New Testament book of Luke. (ESV))

Luke 3:23-38 English Standard Version (ESV)

The Genealogy of Jesus Christ

[23] Jesus, when he began his ministry, was about thirty years of age, being the son (as was supposed) of Joseph, the son of Heli, [24] the son of Matthat, the son of Levi, the son of Melchi, the son of Jannai, the son of Joseph, [25] the son of Mattathias, the son of Amos, the son of Nahum, the son of Esli, the son of Naggai, [26] the son of Maath, the son of Mattathias, the son of Semein, the son of Josech, the son of Joda, [27] the son of Joanan, the son of Rhesa, the son of Zerubbabel, the son of Shealtiel,[a] the son of Neri, [28] the son of Melchi, the son of Addi, the son of Cosam, the son of Elmadam, the son of Er, [29] the son of Joshua, the son of Eliezer, the son of Jorim, the son of Matthat, the son of Levi, [30] the son of Simeon, the son of Judah, the son of Joseph, the son of Jonam, the son of

Eliakim, [31] the son of Melea, the son of Menna, the son of Mattatha, the son of Nathan, the son of David, [32] the son of Jesse, the son of Obed, the son of Boaz, the son of Sala, the son of Nahshon, [33] the son of Amminadab, the son of Admin, the son of Arni, the son of Hezron, the son of Perez, the son of Judah, [34] the son of Jacob, the son of Isaac, the son of Abraham, the son of Terah, the son of Nahor, [35] the son of Serug, the son of Reu, the son of Peleg, the son of Eber, the son of Shelah, [36] the son of Cainan, the son of Arphaxad, the son of Shem, the son of Noah, the son of Lamech, [37] the son of Methuselah, the son of Enoch, the son of Jared, the son of Mahalaleel, the son of Cainan, [38] the son of Enos, the son of Seth, the son of Adam, the son of God.

That's a list of the family lineage. I didn't number them in that chapter. Do you know why?

> "You don't do obvious."

Cheryl Goetz-Ward, you are a GENIUS, and WE NEED YOUR MIND.

> "Yeah… Yeah… Refresh my memory, though… why is that, exactly?"

That question has many answers. For now, you get two:

1) Because this way is much more fun.
2) To confound the wicked.

Puzzle pieces to play with until next time… Doing your homework…

There are 77 names. Jesus is listed twice. As the 49th, only as Jesus

(Yeshua), and also the implied 77th.

You can believe I just added this verse if you want to. Given the state of things, I can see why it might be hard to accept that it's been in there the whole time.

The Parable of the Unforgiving Servant

Matthew 18:21 (ESV)

[21] Then Peter came up and said to him, "Lord, how often will my brother sin against me, and I forgive him? As many as seven times?" [22] Jesus said to him, "I do not say to you seven times, but seventy-seven times.

Reread Samuel I, then tell me again what I can and can't do. Oh, and just for giggles read Luke 1:77

While you're at it, check out 2nd Peter. I was kidding before. That's not new, either.

You'll get a good jump on the third book in this trilogy.

> ***Heartfelt request: Please WHISPER TO YOUR FRIENDS IN SOCIAL MEDIA - TELL THEM THEY HAVE TO READ THIS BOOK. I NEED IT TO GET THIS GENIE OUT OF THE BOTTLE WITH ZERO MARKETING, and I can't initially link it to ANYTHING ELSE. Please leave a great review with a fair amount of profanity… remember… to confound the wicked. Don't be confused if you see a sad, broken link to "Transitions," where this book should be.
>
> With your help, it won't remain that way for very long. If you leave a positive review, you'll get to purchase Too Many Pairs early, at promotional pricing.

Earlier, I revealed a little about my (God's) process. Here are some back-end insights… I don't get to quit. I don't get to give up. This past year really has been pretty awful, looking at it from the outside, but God has made me adequate for whatever this task is… I'm only turning the page. When something doesn't work, I get a new idea, and I try something else, just like Jesus told me to in **The Parable of the Sower.**

To be very clear, I do NOT HAVE ANY VOICES TELLING ME I AM ANYTHING. That's kind of the point, really. Intuitive thought strings are ALWAYS about helping others.

The Gospel According to Thomas

Mark Mattison translation

Prologue

These are the hidden sayings that the living Jesus spoke and Didymos Judas Thomas wrote down.

Saying 1: True Meaning

And he said, "Whoever discovers the meaning of these sayings won't taste death."

Saying 2: Seek and Find

Jesus said, "Whoever seeks shouldn't stop until they find. When they find, they'll be disturbed. When they're disturbed, they'll be [...] amazed, and reign over the All."

Saying 3: Seeking Within

Jesus said, "If your leaders tell you, 'Look, the kingdom is in heaven,' then the birds of heaven will precede you. If they tell you, 'It's in the sea,' then the fish will precede you. Rather, the kingdom is within you and outside of you.

"When you know yourselves, then you'll be known, and you'll realize that you're the children of the living Father. But if you don't know yourselves, then you live in poverty, and you are the poverty."

Saying 4: First and Last

Jesus said, "The older person won't hesitate to ask a little seven-day-old child about the place of life, and they'll live, because many who are first will be last, and they'll become one."

Saying 5: Hidden and Revealed

Jesus said, "Know what's in front of your face, and what's hidden from you will be revealed to you, because there's nothing hidden that won't be revealed."

Saying 6: Public Ritual

His disciples said to him, "Do you want us to fast? And how should we pray? Should we make donations? And what food should we avoid?"

Jesus said, "Don't lie, and don't do what you hate, because everything is revealed in the sight of heaven; for there's nothing hidden that won't be revealed, and nothing covered up that will stay secret."

Saying 7: The Lion and the Human

Jesus said, "Blessed is the lion that's eaten by a human and then becomes human, but how awful for the human who's eaten by a lion, and the lion becomes human."

Saying 8: The Parable of the Fish

He said, "The human being is like a wise fisher who cast a net into the sea and drew it up from the sea full of little fish. Among them the wise fisher found a fine large fish and cast all the little fish back down into the sea, easily choosing the large fish. Anyone who has ears to hear should hear!"

Saying 9: The Parable of the Sower

Jesus said, "Look, a sower went out, took a handful of seeds, and scattered them. Some fell on the roadside; the birds came and gathered them. Others fell on the rock; they didn't take root in the soil and ears of grain didn't rise toward heaven. Yet others fell on thorns; they choked the seeds and worms ate them. Finally, others fell on good soil; it produced fruit up toward heaven, some sixty times as much and some a hundred and twenty."

Saying 10: Jesus and Fire (1)

Jesus said, "I've cast fire on the world, and look, I'm watching over it until it blazes."

Saying 11: Those Who Are Living Won't Die (1)

Jesus said, "This heaven will disappear, and the one above it will disappear too. Those who are dead aren't alive, and those who are living won't die. In the days when you ate what was dead, you made it alive. When you're in the light, what will you do? On the day when you were one, you became divided. But when you become divided, what will you do?"

Saying 12: James the Just

The disciples said to Jesus, "We know you're going to leave us. Who will lead us then?"

Jesus said to them, "Wherever you are, you'll go to James the Just, for whom heaven and earth came into being."

Saying 13: Thomas' Confession

Jesus said to his disciples, "If you were to compare me to someone, who would you say I'm like?"

Simon Peter said to him, "You're like a just angel."

Matthew said to him, "You're like a wise philosopher."

Thomas said to him, "Teacher, I'm completely unable to say whom you're like."

Jesus said, "I'm not your teacher. Because you've drunk, you've become intoxicated by the bubbling spring I've measured out."

He took him aside and told him three things. When Thomas returned to his companions, they asked, "What did Jesus say to you?"

Thomas said to them, "If I tell you one of the things he said to me, you'll pick up stones and cast them at me, and fire will come out of the stones and burn you up."

Saying 14: Public Ministry

Jesus said to them, "If you fast, you'll bring guilt upon yourselves; and if you pray, you'll be condemned; and if you make donations, you'll harm your spirits.

"If they welcome you when you enter any land and go around in the countryside, heal those who are sick among them and eat whatever they give you, because it's not what goes into your mouth that will defile you. What comes out of your mouth is what will defile you."

Saying 15: Worship

Jesus said, "When you see the one who wasn't born of a woman, fall down on your face and worship that person. That's your Father."

Saying 16: Not Peace, but War

Jesus said, "Maybe people think that I've come to cast peace on the world, and they don't know that I've come to cast divisions on the earth: fire, sword, and war. Where there are five in a house, there'll be three against two and two against three, father against and son and son against father. They'll stand up and be one."

Saying 17: Divine Gift

Jesus said, "I'll give you what no eye has ever seen, no ear has ever heard, no hand has ever touched, and no human mind has ever thought."

Saying 18: Beginning and End

The disciples said to Jesus, "Tell us about our end. How will it come?"

Jesus said, "Have you discovered the beginning so that you can look for the end? Because the end will be where the beginning is. Blessed is the one who will stand up in the beginning. They'll know the end, and won't taste death."

Saying 19: Five Trees in Paradise

Jesus said, "Blessed is the one who came into being before coming into being. If you become my disciples and listen to my message, these stones will become your servants; because there are five trees in paradise which don't change in summer or winter, and their leaves don't fall. Whoever knows them won't taste death."

Saying 20: The Parable of the Mustard Seed

The disciples asked Jesus, "Tell us, what can the kingdom of heaven be compared to?"

He said to them, "It can be compared to a mustard seed. Though it's the smallest of all the seeds, when it falls on tilled soil it makes a plant so large that it shelters the birds of heaven."

Saying 21: The Parables of the Field, the Bandits, and the Reaper

Mary said to Jesus, "Whom are your disciples like?"

He said, "They're like little children living in a field which isn't theirs. When the owners of the field come, they'll say, 'Give our field back to us.' They'll strip naked in front of them to let them have it and give them their field.

"So I say that if the owner of the house realizes the bandit is coming, they'll watch out beforehand and won't let the bandit break into the house of their domain and steal their possessions. You, then, watch out for the world! Prepare to defend yourself so that the bandits don't attack you, because what you're expecting will come. May there be a wise person among you!

"When the fruit ripened, the reaper came quickly, sickle in hand, and harvested it. Anyone who has ears to hear should hear!"

Saying 22: Making the Two into One

Jesus saw some little children nursing. He said to his disciples, "These nursing children can be compared to those who enter the kingdom."

They said to him, "Then we'll enter the kingdom as little children?"

Jesus said to them, "When you make the two into one, and make the inner like the outer and the outer like the inner, and the upper like the lower, and so make the male and the female a single one so that the male won't be male nor the female female; when you make eyes in the place of an eye, a hand in the place of a hand, a foot in the place of a foot, and an image in the place of an image; then you'll enter [the kingdom]."

Saying 23: Those Who are Chosen (1)

Jesus said, "I'll choose you, one out of a thousand and two out of ten thousand, and they'll stand as a single one."

Saying 24: Light

His disciples said, "Show us the place where you are, because we need to look for it."

He said to them, "Anyone who has ears to hear should hear! Light exists within a person of light, and they light up the whole world. If they don't shine, there's darkness."

Saying 25: Love and Protect

Jesus said, "Love your brother as your own soul. Protect them like the pupil of your eye."

Saying 26: Speck and Beam

Jesus said, "You see the speck that's in your brother's eye, but you don't see the beam in your own eye. When you get the beam out of your own eye, then you'll be able to see clearly to get the speck out of your brother's eye."

Saying 27: Fasting and Sabbath

"If you don't fast from the world, you won't find the kingdom. If you don't make the Sabbath into a Sabbath, you won't see the

Father."

Saying 28: The World is Drunk

Jesus said, "I stood in the middle of the world and appeared to them in the flesh. I found them all drunk; I didn't find any of them thirsty. My soul ached for the children of humanity, because they were blind in their hearts and couldn't see. They came into the world empty and plan on leaving the world empty. Meanwhile, they're drunk. When they shake off their wine, then they'll change."

Saying 29: Spirit and Body

Jesus said, "If the flesh came into existence because of spirit, that's amazing. If spirit came into existence because of the body, that's really amazing! But I'm amazed at how [such] great wealth has been placed in this poverty."

Saying 30: Divine Presence

Jesus said, "Where there are three deities, they're divine. Where there are two or one, I'm with them."

Saying 31: Prophet and Doctor

Jesus said, "No prophet is welcome in their own village. No doctor heals those who know them."

Saying 32: The Parable of the Fortified City

Jesus said, "A city built and fortified on a high mountain can't fall, nor can it be hidden."

Saying 33: The Parable of the Lamp

Jesus said, "What you hear with one ear, listen to with both, then proclaim from your rooftops. No one lights a lamp and puts it under a basket or in a hidden place. Rather, they put it on the stand so that everyone who comes and goes can see its light."

Saying 34: The Parable of Those Who Can't See

Jesus said, "If someone who's blind leads someone else who's blind, both of them fall into a pit."

Saying 35: The Parable of Binding the Strong

Jesus said, "No one can break into the house of the strong and take it by force without tying the hands of the strong. Then they can loot the house."

Saying 36: Anxiety

Jesus said, "Don't be anxious from morning to evening or from evening to morning about what you'll wear."

Saying 37: Seeing Jesus

His disciples said, "When will you appear to us? When will we see you?"

Jesus said, "When you strip naked without being ashamed, and throw your clothes on the ground and stomp on them as little children would, then [you'll] see the Son of the Living One and won't be afraid."

Saying 38: Finding Jesus

Jesus said, "Often you've wanted to hear this message that I'm telling you, and you don't have anyone else from whom to hear it. There will be days when you'll look for me, but you won't be able to find me."

Saying 39: The Keys of Knowledge

Jesus said, "The Pharisees and the scholars have taken the keys of knowledge and hidden them. They haven't entered, and haven't let others enter who wanted to. So be wise as serpents and innocent as doves."

Saying 40: A Grapevine

Jesus said, "A grapevine has been planted outside of the Father. Since it's malnourished, it'll be pulled up by its root and destroyed."

Saying 41: More and Less

Jesus said, "Whoever has something in hand will be given more, but whoever doesn't have anything will lose even what little they do have."

Saying 42: Passing By

Jesus said, "Become passersby."

Saying 43: The Tree and the Fruit

His disciples said to him, "Who are you to say these things to us?"

"You don't realize who I am from what I say to you, but you've become like those Judeans who either love the tree but hate its fruit, or love the fruit but hate the tree."

Saying 44: Blasphemy

Jesus said, "Whoever blasphemes the Father will be forgiven, and whoever blasphemes the Son will be forgiven, but whoever blasphemes the Holy Spirit will not be forgiven, neither on earth nor in heaven."

Saying 45: Good and Evil

Jesus said, "Grapes aren't harvested from thorns, nor are figs gathered from thistles, because they don't produce fruit. [A person who's good] brings good things out of their treasure, and a person who's [evil] brings evil things out of their evil treasure. They say evil things because their heart is full of evil."

Saying 46: Greater than John the Baptizer

Jesus said, "From Adam to John the Baptizer, no one's been born who's so much greater than John the Baptizer that they shouldn't avert their eyes. But I say that whoever among you will become a little child will know the kingdom and become greater than John."

Saying 47: The Parables of Divided Loyalties, New Wine in Old Wineskins, and New Patch on Old Cloth

Jesus said, "It's not possible for anyone to mount two horses or stretch two bows, and it's not possible for a servant to follow two leaders, because they'll respect one and despise the other.

"No one drinks old wine and immediately wants to drink new wine. And new wine isn't put in old wineskins, because they'd burst. Nor is old wine put in new wineskins, because it'd spoil.

"A new patch of cloth isn't sewn onto an old coat, because it'd tear apart."

Saying 48: Unity (1)

Jesus said, "If two make peace with each other in a single house, they'll say to the mountain, 'Go away,' and it will."

Saying 49: Those Who Are Chosen (2)

Jesus said, "Blessed are those who are one – those who are chosen, because you'll find the kingdom. You've come from there and will return there."

Saying 50: Our Origin and Identity

Jesus said, "If they ask you, 'Where do you come from?' tell them, 'We've come from the light, the place where light came into being by itself, [established] itself, and appeared in their image.'

"If they ask you, 'Is it you?' then say, 'We are its children, and we're chosen by our living Father.'

"If they ask you, 'What's the sign of your Father in you?' then say, 'It's movement and rest.'"

Saying 51: The New World

His disciples said to him, "When will the dead have rest, and when will the new world come?"

He said to them, "What you're looking for has already come, but you don't know it."

Saying 52: Twenty-Four Prophets

His disciples said to him, "Twenty-four prophets have spoken in

Israel, and they all spoke of you."

He said to them, "You've ignored the Living One right in front of you, and you've talked about those who are dead."

Saying 53: True Circumcision

His disciples said to him, "Is circumcision useful, or not?"

He said to them, "If it were useful, parents would have children who are born circumcised. But the true circumcision in spirit has become profitable in every way."

Saying 54: Those Who Are Poor

Jesus said, "Blessed are those who are poor, for yours is the kingdom of heaven."

Saying 55: Discipleship (1)

Jesus said, "Whoever doesn't hate their father and mother can't become my disciple, and whoever doesn't hate their brothers and sisters and take up their cross like I do isn't worthy of me."

Saying 56: The World is a Corpse

Jesus said, "Whoever has known the world has found a corpse. Whoever has found a corpse, of them the world isn't worthy."

Saying 57: The Parable of the Weeds

Jesus said, "My Fathers' kingdom can be compared to someone who had [good] seed. Their enemy came by night and sowed weeds among the good seed. The person didn't let anyone pull out the weeds, 'so that you don't pull out the wheat along with the weeds,' they said to them. 'On the day of the harvest, the weeds will be obvious. Then they'll be pulled out and burned.'"

Saying 58: Finding Life

Jesus said, "Blessed is the person who's gone to a lot of trouble. They've found life."

Saying 59: The Living One

Jesus said, "Look for the Living One while you're still alive. If you die and then try to look for him, you won't be able to."

Saying 60: Don't Become a Corpse

They saw a Samaritan carrying a lamb to Judea. He said to his disciples, "What do you think he's going to do with that lamb?"

They said to him, "He's going to kill it and eat it."

He said to them, "While it's living, he won't eat it, but only after he kills it and it becomes a corpse."

They said, "He can't do it any other way."

He said to them, "You, too, look for a resting place, so that you won't become a corpse and be eaten."

Saying 61: Jesus and Salome

Jesus said, "Two will rest on a couch. One will die, the other will live."

Salome said, "Who are you, Sir, to climb onto my couch and eat off my table as if you're from someone?"

Jesus said to her, "I'm the one who exists in equality. Some of what belongs to my Father was given to me."

"I'm your disciple."

"So I'm telling you, if someone is /equal\, they'll be full of light; but if they're divided, they'll be full of darkness."

Saying 62: Mysteries

Jesus said, "I tell my mysteries to [those who are worthy of my] mysteries. Don't let your left hand know what your right hand is doing."

Saying 63: The Parable of the Rich Fool

Jesus said, "There was a rich man who had much money. He said, 'I'll use my money to sow, reap, plant, and fill my barns with fruit, so that I won't need anything.' That's what he was thinking to himself, but he died that very night. Anyone who has ears to hear should hear!"

Saying 64: The Parable of the Dinner Party

Jesus said, "Someone was planning on having guests. When dinner was ready, they sent their servant to call the visitors.

"The servant went to the first and said, 'My master invites you.'

"They said, 'Some merchants owe me money. They're coming tonight. I need to go and give them instructions. Excuse me from the dinner.'

"The servant went to another one and said, 'My master invites you.'

"They said, "I've just bought a house and am needed for the day.

I won't have time.'

"The servant went to another one and said, 'My master invites you.'

"They said, 'My friend is getting married and I'm going to make dinner. I can't come. Excuse me from the dinner.'

"The servant went to another one and said, 'My master invites you.'

"They said, "I've just bought a farm and am going to collect the rent. I can't come. Excuse me.'

"The servant went back and told the master, 'The ones you've invited to the dinner have excused themselves.'

"The master said to their servant, 'Go out to the roads and bring whomever you find so that they can have dinner.'

"Buyers and merchants won't [enter] the places of my Father."

Saying 65: The Parable of the Sharecroppers

He said, "A [creditor] owned a vineyard. He leased it out to some sharecroppers to work it so he could collect its fruit.

"He sent his servant so that the sharecroppers could give him the fruit of the vineyard. They seized his servant, beat him, and nearly killed him.

"The servant went back and told his master. His master said, 'Maybe he just didn't know them.' He sent another servant, but the tenants beat that one too.

"Then the master sent his son, thinking, 'Maybe they'll show some respect to my son.'

"Because they knew that he was the heir of the vineyard, the sharecroppers seized and killed him. Anyone who has ears to hear should hear!"

Saying 66: The Rejected Cornerstone

Jesus said, "Show me the stone the builders rejected; that's the cornerstone."

Saying 67: Knowing Isn't Everything

Jesus said, "Whoever knows everything, but is personally lacking, lacks everything."

Saying 68: Persecution

Jesus said, "Blessed are you when you're hated and persecuted, and no place will be found where you've been persecuted."

Saying 69: Those Who Are Persecuted

Jesus said, "Blessed are those who've been persecuted in their own hearts. They've truly known the Father. Blessed are those who are hungry, so that their stomachs may be filled."

Saying 70: Salvation is Within

Jesus said, "If you give birth to what's within you, what you have within you will save you. If you don't have that within [you], what you don't have within you [will] kill you."

Saying 71: Destroying the Temple

Jesus said, "I'll destroy [this] house, and no one will be able to build it [...]"

Saying 72: Not a Divider

[Someone said to him], "Tell my brothers to divide our inheritance with me."

He said to him, "Who made me a divider?"

He turned to his disciples and said to them, "Am I really a divider?"

Saying 73: Workers for the Harvest

Jesus said, "The harvest really is plentiful, but the workers are few. So pray that the Lord will send workers to the harvest."

Saying 74: The Empty Well

He said, "Lord, many are gathered around the well, but there's nothing to drink."

Saying 75: The Bridal Chamber

Jesus said, "Many are waiting at the door, but those who are one will enter the bridal chamber."

Saying 76: The Parable of the Pearl

Jesus said, "The Father's kingdom can be compared to a merchant with merchandise who found a pearl. The merchant was wise; they sold their merchandise and bought that single pearl for themselves.

"You, too, look for the treasure that doesn't perish but endures, where no moths come to eat and no worms destroy."

Saying 77: Jesus is the All

Jesus said, "I'm the light that's over all. I am the All. The All has come from me and unfolds toward me.

"Split a log; I'm there. Lift the stone, and you'll find me there."

Saying 78: Into the Desert

Jesus said, "What did you go out into the desert to see? A reed shaken by the wind? A [person] wearing fancy clothes, [like your] rulers and powerful people? They (wear) fancy [clothes], but can't know the truth."

Saying 79: Listening to the Message

A woman in the crowd said to him, "Blessed is the womb that bore you, and the breasts that nourished you."

He said to [her], "Blessed are those who have listened to the message of the Father and kept it, because there will be days when you'll say, 'Blessed is the womb that didn't conceive and the breasts that haven't given milk.'"

Saying 80: The World is a Body

Jesus said, "Whoever has known the world has found the body; but whoever has found the body, of them the world isn't worthy."

Saying 81: Riches and Renunciation (1)

Jesus said, "Whoever has become rich should become a ruler, and whoever has power should renounce it."

Saying 82: Jesus and Fire (2)

Jesus said, "Whoever is near me is near the fire, and whoever is far from me is far from the kingdom."

Saying 83: Light and Images

Jesus said, "Images are revealed to people, but the light within them is hidden in the image of the Father's light. He'll be revealed, but his image will be hidden by his light."

Saying 84: Our Previous Images

Jesus said, "When you see your likeness, you rejoice. But when you see your images that came into being before you did –

which don't die, and aren't revealed – how much you'll have to bear!"

Saying 85: Adam Wasn't Worthy

Jesus said, "Adam came into being from a great power and great wealth, but he didn't become worthy of you. If he had been worthy, [he wouldn't have tasted] death."

Saying 86: Foxes and Birds

Jesus said, "[The foxes have dens] and the birds have nests, but the Son of Humanity has nowhere to lay his head and rest."

Saying 87: Body and Soul

Jesus said, "How miserable is the body that depends on a body, and how miserable is the soul that depends on both."

Saying 88: Angels and Prophets

Jesus said, "The angels and the prophets will come to you and give you what belongs to you. You'll give them what you have and ask yourselves, 'When will they come and take what is theirs?'"

Saying 89: Inside and Outside

Jesus said, "Why do you wash the outside of the cup? Don't you know that whoever created the inside created the outside too?"

Saying 90: Jesus' Yoke is Easy

Jesus said, "Come to me, because my yoke is easy and my requirements are light. You'll be refreshed."

Saying 91: Reading the Signs

They said to him, "Tell us who you are so that we may trust you."

He said to them, "You read the face of the sky and the earth, but you don't know the one right in front of you, and you don't know how to read the present moment."

Saying 92: Look and Find

Jesus said, "Look and you'll find. I didn't answer your questions before. Now I want to give you answers, but you aren't looking for them."

Saying 93: Don't Throw Pearls to Pigs

"Don't give what's holy to the dogs, or else it might be thrown on the manure pile. Don't throw pearls to the pigs, or else they might […]"

Saying 94: Knock and It Will Be Opened

Jesus [said], "Whoever looks will find, [and whoever knocks], it will be opened for them."

Saying 95: Giving Money

[Jesus said], "If you have money, don't lend it at interest. Instead, give [it to] someone from whom you won't get it back."

Saying 96: The Parable of the Yeast

Jesus [said], "The Father's kingdom can be compared to a woman who took a little yeast and [hid] it in flour. She made it into large loaves of bread. Anyone who has ears to hear should hear!"

Saying 97: The Parable of the Jar of Flour

Jesus said, "The Father's kingdom can be compared to a woman carrying a jar of flour. While she was walking down [a] long road, the jar's handle broke and the flour spilled out behind her on the road. She didn't know it, and didn't realize there was a problem until she got home, put down the jar, and found it empty."

Saying 98: The Parable of the Assassin

Jesus said, "The Father's kingdom can be compared to a man who wanted to kill someone powerful. He drew his sword in his house and drove it into the wall to figure out whether his hand was strong enough. Then he killed the powerful one."

Saying 99: Jesus' True Family

The disciples said to him, "Your brothers and mother are standing outside."

He said to them, "The people here who do the will of my Father are my brothers and mother; they're the ones who will enter my Father's kingdom."

Saying 100: Give to Caesar What Belongs to Caesar

They showed Jesus a gold coin and said to him, "Those who

belong to Caesar demand tribute from us."

He said to them, "Give to Caesar what belongs to Caesar, give to God what belongs to God, and give to me what belongs to me."

Saying 101: Discipleship (2)

"Whoever doesn't hate their [father] and mother as I do can't become my [disciple], and whoever [doesn't] love their [father] and mother as I do can't become my [disciple]. For my mother […], but [my] true [Mother] gave me Life."

Saying 102: The Dog in the Feeding Trough

Jesus said, "How awful for the Pharisees who are like a dog sleeping in a feeding trough for cattle, because the dog doesn't eat, and [doesn't let] the cattle eat either."

Saying 103: The Parable of the Bandits

Jesus said, "Blessed is the one who knows where the bandits are going to enter. [They can] get up to assemble their defenses and be prepared to defend themselves before they arrive."

Saying 104: Prayer and Fasting

They said to [Jesus], "Come, let's pray and fast today."

Jesus said, "What have I done wrong? Have I failed?

"Rather, when the groom leaves the bridal chamber, then people should fast and pray."

Saying 105: Knowing Father and Mother

Jesus said, "Whoever knows their father and mother will be called a bastard."

Saying 106: Unity (2)

Jesus said, "When you make the two into one, you'll become Children of Humanity, and if you say 'Mountain, go away!', it'll go."

Saying 107: The Parable of the Lost Sheep

Jesus said, "The kingdom can be compared to a shepherd who had a hundred sheep. The largest one strayed. He left the ninety-nine and looked for that one until he found it. Having gone through the trouble, he said to the sheep: 'I love you more than the ninety-nine.'"

Saying 108: Becoming Like Jesus

Jesus said, "Whoever drinks from my mouth will become like me, and I myself will become like them; then, what's hidden will be revealed to them."

Saying 109: The Parable of the Hidden Treasure

Jesus said, "The kingdom can be compared to someone who had a treasure [hidden] in their field. [They] didn't know about it. After they died, they left it to their son. The son didn't know it either. He took the field and sold it.

"The buyer plowed the field, [found] the treasure, and began to loan money at interest to whomever they wanted."

Saying 110: Riches and Renunciation (2)

Jesus said, "Whoever has found the world and become rich should renounce the world."

Saying 111: Those Who are Living Won't Die (2)

Jesus said, "The heavens and the earth will roll up in front of you, and whoever lives from the Living One won't see death."

Doesn't Jesus say, "Whoever finds themselves, of them the world isn't worthy"?

Saying 112: Flesh and Soul

Jesus said, "How awful for the flesh that depends on the soul. How awful for the soul that depends on the flesh."

Saying 113: The Kingdom is Already Present

His disciples said to him, "When will the kingdom come?"

"It won't come by looking for it. They won't say, 'Look over here!' or 'Look over there!' Rather, the Father's kingdom is already spread out over the earth, and people don't see it."

Saying 114: Peter and Mary

Simon Peter said to them, "Mary should leave us, because women aren't worthy of life."

Jesus said, "Look, am I to make her a man? So that she may become a living spirit too, she's equal to you men, because every woman who makes herself manly will enter the kingdom of heaven."

Z